SPALDING

BASKETBALL
INBOUND ATTACK

Tom Reiter

mp

MASTERS PRESS

A Division of Howard W. Sams & Co.

Published by Masters Press (A Division of Howard W. Sams & Co.)
2647 Waterfront Pkwy E. Dr.
Suite 300
Indianapolis, IN 46214

First printing, March 1993.
Second printing, October 1993.

Printed in the United States of America

Library of Congress Cataloging-in-Publication Data
Reiter, Tom, 1953-
   Spalding Basketball Inbound Attack/Tom Reiter
      p.   cm. — (Spalding sports library)
   ISBN 0-940279-60-6
   1. Basketball—Offense. 2. Basketball—Training. I. Title
   II. Title: Basketball inbound attack. III. Series.
GV889.R43   1993   93-12084
796.323'2–dc20   CIP

Credits

Editor: Mark Montieth
Cover design: Julie Biddle
Cover photograph: Brian Spurlock, Spurlock Photography, Inc.
                  Indianapolis, Ind.

To my wife, Stacie, and my sons, Matt and Dan.
Without their patience and sacrifice, I could never have been a coach.

To Rick Majerus, who taught me how the game should be played.

To Gene Keady, who gave me the opportunity of a lifetime.

"There is no such thing as a successful defense."

— *General George S. Patton*

Contents

Foreword

Basketball Inbound Attack is the only book I know of that deals with a crucial aspect of the game that has long been overlooked — the out-of-bounds play. Tom Reiter has compiled an outstanding book in this regard that is thorough, pays attention to detail and yet can be easily understood by player and coach alike.

The plays, sets and formations are applicable at absolutely every level. It has been my good fortune to coach in grade school, high school, college and professional ball, and I have found something that can be of use at every level within the context of this book.

Tom is an outstanding coach in his own right. He has worked for one of the finest coaches in America, Gene Keady, for seven years, and this book draws upon his experience and knowledge. From a defensive standpoint alone I would want this book, because it would help me to better understand how to eliminate the easy score under the basket. I also must confess that I've already stolen a play or two that I am proud to have incorporated in my offensive end-out attack at the University of Utah. All coaches should enjoy the mental gymnastics of the challenges that each play presents for both the offense and defense.

Coaches who buy this book will be glad they did. After all, it might turn out to be a small price to pay for victory.

RICK MAJERUS
Head Coach, University of Utah

Preface

There are as many philosophies about how basketball should be played as there are coaches. Some are offense-oriented, wanting to run and increase the tempo with a fast-paced attack in an effort to overwhelm opponents. Others put more emphasis on defense, trying to create scoring opportunities out of sheer tenacity. All coaches, however, have one thing in common: they want to score points!

This collection of inbound plays helps them do that. Although it does not include every possible method if inbounding the ball in the offensive court, it represents years of watching basketball and talking with other coaches at summer camps and clinics. While scouting countless games, I have seen teams win games with a last-second inbound play, and I have seen teams lose games for lack of one.

Some teams have several inbound plays, others have one or two and others just want to get the ball inbounds and set up their offense. Most coaches agree, however, that having the ball so close to their basket and the chance to set up an open shot with one or more passes is an opportunity to be taken seriously.

Think of all the hours teams practice their halfcourt offense during the season. Isn't it a logical extension, then, to emphasize the beginning of the offense so close to the offensive basket? Every coach looks for easy ways to score, and inbound plays afford that opportunity.

I have tried to include plays that fit into any offensive system — box sets, stack sets, baseline sets and miscellaneous, or random, sets. Some plays are intended to create interior scoring opportunities and others try to set up three-point shots. I have assigned the traditional numbers to each position — 1 to the point guard, 2 to the shooting guard, 3 to the small forward, 4 to the power forward and 5 to the center. Coaches, however, must utilize their players where they believe they will be most effective.

Certain factors improve a play's effectiveness, regardless of its design. First and foremost is execution. Sharp cuts are a necessity. Staggered screening, in which two screeners get a cutter open by screening in a staggered sequence, is an effective means of getting a cutter open for a shot. Having a big man screen for a perimeter player also improves a play's chance of success. "Pick the picker" plays, in which the player being screened for turns and screens for the player who just screened for him, force the defense to decide whether or not to switch. An effective variation includes moving the post players to the perimeter to spread the defense and having them cut off of screens to the basket after the ball has been reversed.

Coaches must understand that their team has a rare opportunity to control the game when it is taking the ball out of bounds at its end of the court. Serious practice preparation should be devoted to improving these opportunities.

Teams average at least eight inbound plays at the offensive end of their court per game. Successful execution of only half of them adds at least eight points, more if three-point field goals or three-point plays are executed. What coach can't use an extra eight points per game?

Obviously, it would be impossible to make every play in this book part of your system, but incorporating those that enable you to make the best use of your personnel can lead to an easy basket now and then — perhaps even get you a game-winner. Take advantage!

Key to Diagrams

1, 2, 3, 4, 5   Offensive players

X_1, X_2, X_3, X_4, X_5 Defensive players

◯   Offensive player with the ball

   Pass

                                                Dribble

Cut made by an offensive player

   Pivot made by an offensive player

Box Sets

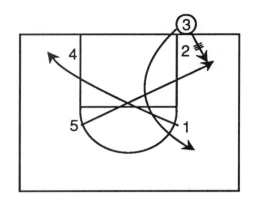

A

Players #1 and #5 cross out, with #5 receiving the inbound pass. Player #3 empties out to isolate #2 on the block.

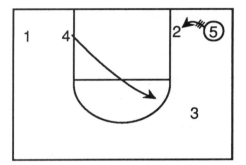

B

After #3 cuts to the perimeter, #4 flashes to the high post. Player #1 widens out to the three-point line on the weak side.

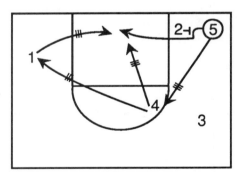

C

Player #5 passes to #4 and #2 steps out to backscreen for a shuffle cut for #5. Player #4 can pass to #5 in the lane or can reverse the ball to #1 for a pass to #5 in the low post.

D

Option: If #4 is covered on the flash cut, #5 passes to #3. Player #5 then screens in for #2 for a shot or a post feed back to #5.

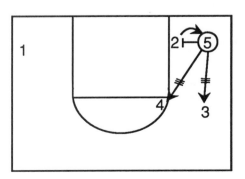

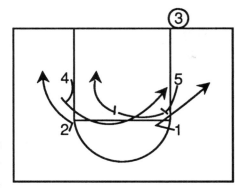

A

Both post players screen up the lane for the guards. The guards cut hard toward the baseline for the quick inbound pass. Both of the guards must set up their defenders before their cut to the baseline.

After the guards cut, player #5 screens #4's defender. If the defense switches, #5 rolls back to the ball with the defender out of position.

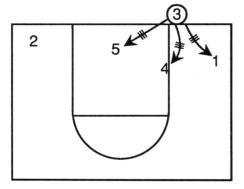

B

Player #1 can either shoot the ball after catching it or look inside for the quick interior pass.

C

If #3 passes to #1, both #4 and #5 screen for the inbounder. Player #1 passes to #3 for a scoring opportunity.

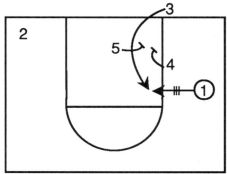

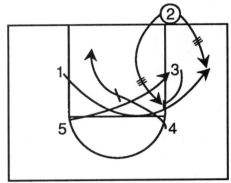

A

Players #4 and #5 cross in the lane, with #4 attempting to get in the way of #5's defender.

Player #3 curls to the free throw line to screen for #1, who is coming to the ball-side wing. Player #3 then turns toward the ball for a possible pass from #2.

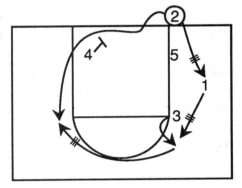

B

If #2 inbounds to #1, the ball gets reversed and #4 screens for #2, who empties out to the weak-side wing.

C

The ball is reversed to #2, who looks for the shot first, then for a low post feed to #4.

Player #5 flashes high. If the pass is received, #5 can shoot or look for the high/low pass to #4.

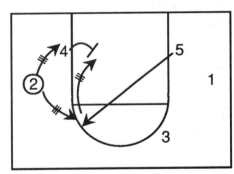

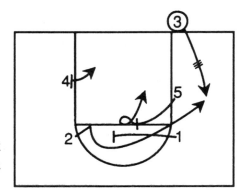

A

This is an effective play to either get the ball inbounded safely or to get a quick jump shot.

Player #1 and #5 set staggered screens for #2, who cuts hard to the ball for a shot. Player #5 then turns back to the ball for a lob pass in the lane. Player #4 ducks into the lane looking for a possible bounce pass.

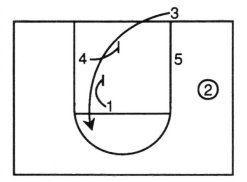

B

If #2 doesn't take the jump shot, #5 posts up for a two-player game while #3 receives a double screen from both #4 and #1.

4

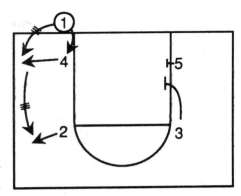

A

Player #4 steps out to the corner to receive the inbound pass. After #4 catches it, the inbounder (#1) steps in hard to post up for a return pass from #4.

Players #3 and #5 tighten up on the weak-side block for a double screen. If #4 reverses the ball to #2, #1 steps out and backscreens for #4.

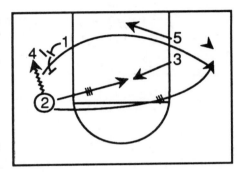

B

Option: If #1 does not receive the pass from #4, #1 screens for #4 and then continues out to the perimeter to screen for #2. Player #4 cuts underneath the weak-side double screen for a skip pass.

Player #3 flashes to the ball after #4 cuts underneath, and #5 ducks to the basket to seal the defender for a possible lob.

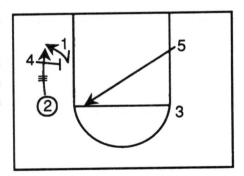

C

Option: Player #4 screens in for #1 and then posts up. Player #5 flashes to the ball to eliminate weak-side defensive help.

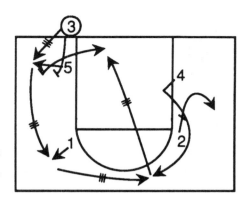

A

The emphasis of this play is a lob pass to a big player cutting along the baseline, but it includes many other options.

Player #5 steps out for the inbound pass from #3. The ball is reversed to #1 and then to #4. After #2 screens down for #4, #3 backscreens for #5 and #4 throws a lob pass to #5.

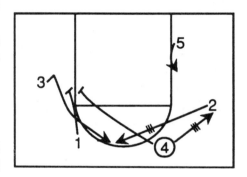

B

If the lob pass is not thrown to #5, #4 reverses the ball to #2. Then both #1 and #4 screen down for #3, who looks for the jump shot. While this is developing, #5 is posting up looking for a pass from #2.

C

If #3 catches the ball at the top of the key but is unable to shoot, #5 flashes to the free throw line and #2 goes back-door.

Player #3 also can look to the weak side as #4 screens in for #1. Player #1 can either shoot or look inside to #4.

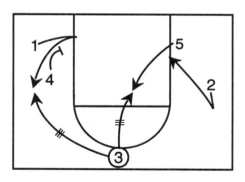

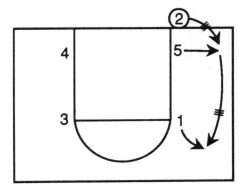

A

Player #5 cuts to the corner for the inbound pass. The ball is reversed to #1.

B

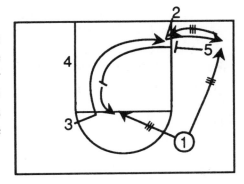

After the ball is passed to #1, #5 cuts toward the lane looking to screen for the inbounder, #2. Player #2 can shoot or can wait as #5 continues to screen for #3 as #3 posts up. If #5 and #3's defenders switch, #5 turns back to the ball in the lane for a short jump shot.

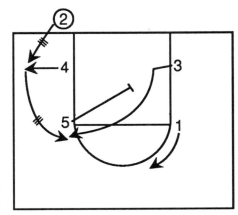

A

Player #4 goes to the corner to receive the inbound pass. At the same time, #5 screens diagonally for #3 for a jump shot. If the defense switches, #5 posts up in the lane against the mismatch.

B

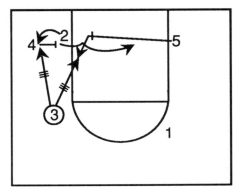

If #3 catches the ball but does not shoot, #4 screens in for the inbounder (#2) for a possible shot. If #3 holds the ball for the next screen, #5 screens #4's defender and #4 cuts into the lane over the top of the screen looking for the ball. Player #5's defender may help on #4, which makes #5 a primary receiver in the low post.

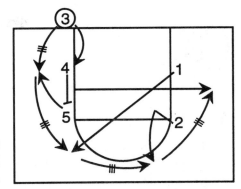

A

This play is especially effective if the inbounder is able to post up or is a good one-on-one player. It is good for a perimeter player who can score inside.

Player #4 screens up the lane for #5 and then clears wide opposite. If the defense switches, the screener must roll back to the ball. Player #1 flashes high to the ball side for a reversal pass from #4.

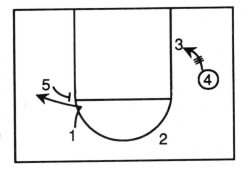

The ball is reversed around the perimeter and #3 is isolated in the lane looking for the pass.

B

Player #4 post feeds #3 as #5 sets a flare screen for #1 and the weak-side players occupy the defense by screening or spotting up on the perimeter.

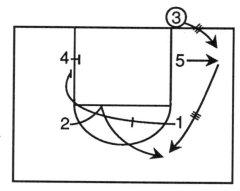

A

This is another play in the series of plays meant to free the inbounder.

Player #5 steps out to the corner to receive the inbound pass from #3. Player #1 screens for #2, who cuts to the ball-side wing to receive the reversal pass from #5. Players #1 and #4 stack on the weak side.

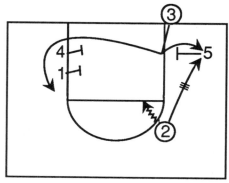

B

Player #2 can pass to #3 off of the screen by #5, or #3 can clear out to the opposite side of the floor looking for a pass over the top of the defense.

Player #2 also can take the ball on the dribble to the basket.

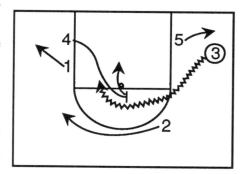

C

Player #3 can dribble into the lane while #2 spots up for a possible jump shot. Player #4 runs a pick-and-roll, which gives #3 a chance to turn the corner for a layup.

Player #1 flares to the corner to spread the defense, while #5 steps away from the lane and reads the position of the players.

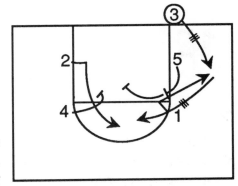

A

Player #5 screens for #1, who cuts to the wing to receive the inbound pass. Players #4 and #5 set a double screen for #2, who is cutting from the opposite block for the jump shot. Player #5 turns back to the ball after screening.

B

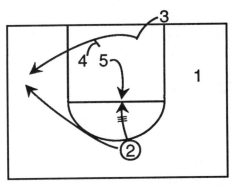

As the play continues, #4 screens for the inbounder and #3 cuts to the wing for a shot on the wing. Player #5 posts in the lane quickly.

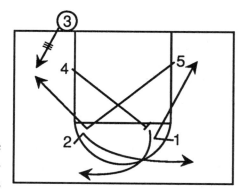

A

The object in this play is to get the defense spread with the perimeter players on the weak side. Player #5 screens diagonally and then cuts to the wing for the initial inbound pass. Player #4 also screens opposite.

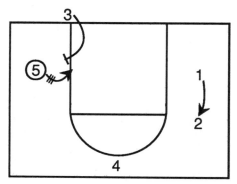

B

Player #5 receives the inbound pass and then #3, the inbounder, steps in to post up for a return pass.

C

If #5 cannot pass to #3 in the low post, #2 backscreens for #4 at the high post.

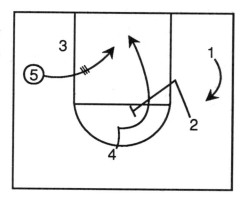

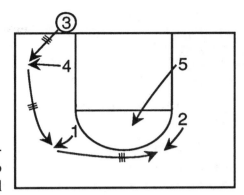

A

Player #4 steps out to receive the inbound pass and reverses it to #1, who passes to #2. Player #5 flashes to the ball looking for a pass. This draws the weakside defense away from the basket.

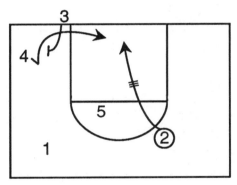

B

The inbounder, #3, backscreens #4's defender and #4 cuts into the lane for a lob pass to the basket from #2. Player #2 may have to dribble to create a better angle for the lob pass.

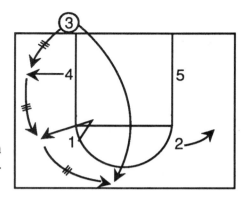

A

This play is effective for teams with dominant inside players who can individually overpower the opponent.

Player #4 steps out to receive the inbound pass. Player #5 follows to the ball-side block to post up for a pass. The inbounder, #3, cuts to the top of the key as the ball is reversed. This empties out the baseline so that #4 and #5 can go two-on-two.

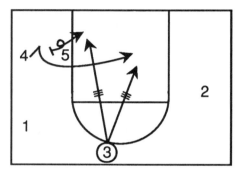

B

Player #5 steps out off of the lane line to backscreen #4's defender. Player #4 shuffle cuts hard across the lane. Player #5 then turns toward the basket looking to duck into the lane for a post-up. Perimeter players spot up for their shots.

This play does not utilize the risky lob pass as a threat to score, and puts pressure on the baseline defenders guarding #4 and #5. If the defense switches, #5 should turn toward the basket and seal. If no switch takes place (and #5 has set a solid screen), #4 should end up being a step or two ahead of the defender for a layup.

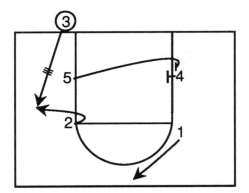

A

This play is ordinarily used against a zone defense, and while simple in its construction, is very effective.

Player #2 cuts to receive the inbound pass as #5 moves opposite the ball across the lane to set a double screen with #4. Both #4 and #5 face in toward the lane.

B

Player #2 reverses the ball to #1. Player #3 cuts around the double screen into the lane. Player #3 usually is not open, but draws the defense. The primary receiver, #5, follows the decoy and then "floods" the zone right behind #3 and receives the pass from #1 in the lane for a short jump shot.

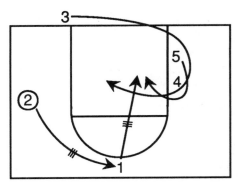

15

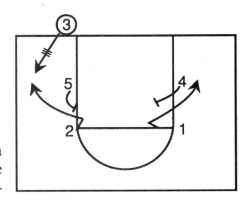

A

This is an excellent play against a man-to-man defense because of the number of potential scoring opportunities it offers.

Player #5 screens up the lane for #2, and #4 does the same thing on the weak side screening for #1.

B

After #2 catches, #3 screens in the lane for #4, who cuts to the ball-side block looking to post up. Player #5, in turn, picks the picker and screens for #3 for the jump shot.

This is an effective play for both the post-up and the jump shot.

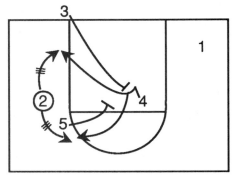

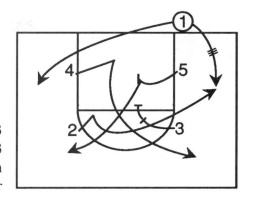

A

Player #2 cuts off of a screen by #3 to take the inbound pass. Both #5 and #3 screen in the lane for #4, who cuts from the block toward the perimeter. Player #5 screens and then pops out to the top of the key. Player #1 passes to #2, and then empties out to the weak side.

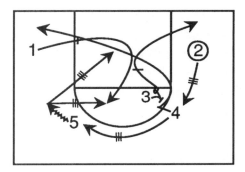

B

The ball is passed around the perimeter from #2 to #4 to #5. As #5 dribbles toward #1, #5 looks to see if #4 gets open off of #3's pick at the foul line. If #4 is not open at the block, #1 also screens for #4. This forces #1's defender to momentarily help on #4. Player #3, who is at the free throw line, turns to screen down the lane, this time for #1, who looks for the jump shot.

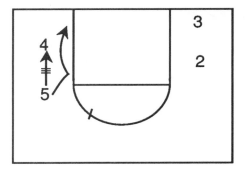

C

Player #4 continues toward the corner if a pass is not available in the low post. If #5 passes to #4 in the corner, #5 cuts to the block looking for the return pass. After #3 has screened for #1, #3 empties out to the other side of the floor.

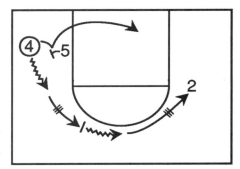

D

The ball is reversed around the perimeter, and #4 receives a backscreen along the baseline from #5.

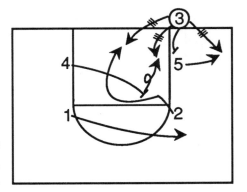

A

Player #4 diagonally screens in the lane for #2. The offense is looking for a defensive switch by #2's and #4's defenders. This leaves a guard defending a big player. Player #5, who is lined up in front of the ball, steps hard to the corner for the inbound pass. Player #3 then steps in for the post-up.

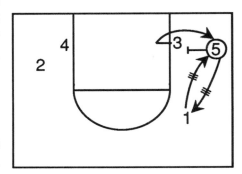

B

If #5 cannot post feed #3 at the block, #5 reverses the ball to #1 and then screens #3's defender for a jump shot along the baseline.

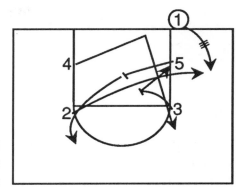

A

Players #5 and #3 set a double screen for #2, who cuts toward the ball for the initial pass. Player #4 cuts to the ball-side wing from the original spot on the opposite block. After #3 screens for #2, #3 comes back toward the ball. Player #5, like #4 steps out on the perimeter.

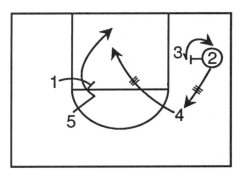

B

Player #2 reverses the ball to #4. At this time, #1 slides up the lane and looks to backscreen #5's defender as #5 shuffle cuts to the basket. If #5's defender does not come out on the perimeter to guard #5, then #1 can backscreen #5's defender for a possible lob pass from #4. At the same time, #2 is screening in for #3 at the block in order to occupy the defense.

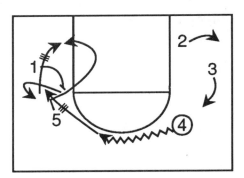

C

Option: If neither of the potential receivers are open, #4 dribbles toward #1 (who had screened for #5). Player #1 steps out on the perimeter and receives a pass from #4. Player #5 curls back for an isolation on the block for the post feed.

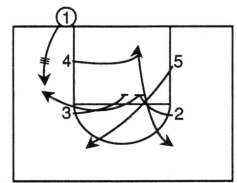

A

Players #2 and #3 screen for #5, who cuts to the top of the key. After #2 screens for #5, #2 cuts to the ball-side wing for the pass from #1. Player #4 slides across the lane looking for a pass from the inbounder. If the pass is not available, #4 also empties out to the perimeter.

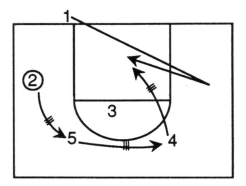

B

Player #2 passes to #5, who reverses the ball to #4. Player #1 cuts to the wing. If a pass is not available, #1 cuts backdoor on the clearout and gets a layup.

C

If #1 is not closely guarded, #4 can make the pass to the wing. Player #5 remains stationary until seeing how the defense is playing #1. If #1 catches the ball on the wing, #5 cuts off of #3 on a shuffle cut to the hoop.

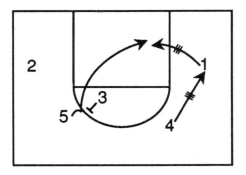

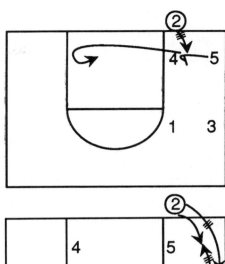

A

Player #4 loops in front of the defense — this cut is made primarily to occupy the defense. Player #5 cuts toward the block, as if to set a screen for #4, but after getting in front of the ball #5 quickly reverse pivots with a drop step and looks for a bounce pass from the inbounder. Player #5 wants to seal the defender and post up.

B

At the same time, #3 screens in for #1, who cuts to the wing for a jump shot. Also, if #1 catches the ball out on the wing, #2 can sneak inbounds for a quick return pass underneath #5 for a shot.

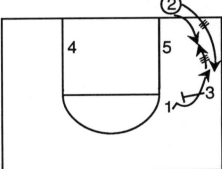

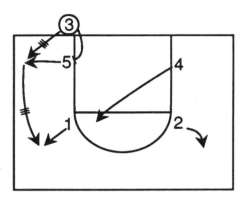

A

Player #5 cuts to the corner for the inbound pass. The inbounder steps in for a quick return pass. Player #4 flashes to the free throw line to eliminate the weakside defense.

B

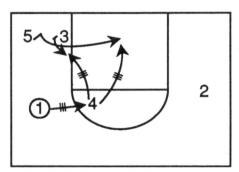

Player #1 passes to #4 and #3 backscreens for #5, who cuts into the lane. If the defense switches, there is a mismatch with #3's defender guarding #5.

C

If the defense is successful in defending the baseline cut, #4 can reverse the ball to #2 and screen down for #3 for a shot at the free throw line.

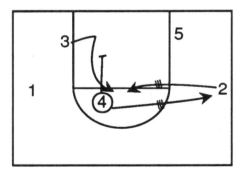

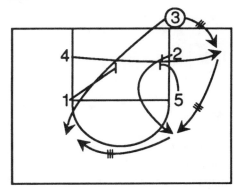

A

This is an effective play with many options.

Players #2 and #5 screen for #4, who cuts across the lane for the inbound pass. Player #2 then peels out to the perimeter for a pass from #4. Player #1 screens in the lane for #3, the inbounder, for a shot off of the ball reversal from #2.

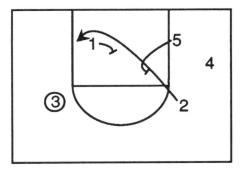

B

After #2 passes to #3, both #5 and #1 set staggered screens for #2, who may get a post-up or who can continue out to the wing.

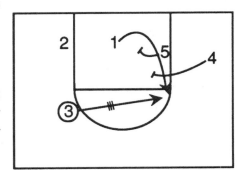

C

After #1 screens for #2, both #4 and #5 screen for #1 for a jump shot. Player #1 is usually open because the defender helps on #2.

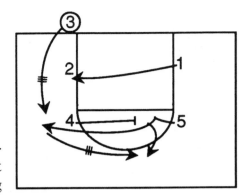

A

Player #4 screens for #5 for the inbound pass. (*Option:* Player #4 can set up the defender by cutting and replacing to receive the inbound pass.)

Player #1 comes across the lane to stack up with #2. Player #5 passes to #4.

B

Players #1 and #5 screen for #2 on a curl move into the lane. Player #3 has the side cleared out for a backdoor cut if closely guarded.

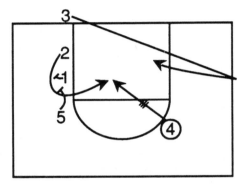

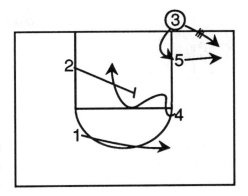

A

Player #5 cuts to the corner for the inbound pass, and #3 steps in to post up for a return pass. Player #2 then back-screens for #4 for a potential lob. If #5 passes to #2 at the free throw line, #2 can either shoot or post feed #4, who turns and pivot in the lane.

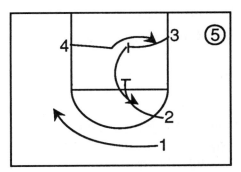

B

Option: If #3 cannot receive the inbound pass and #2 does not receive the pass at the free throw line, #3 turns and screens for #4, who comes to the ball-side block. Player #2 then screens down for #3 as #3 comes to the free throw line.

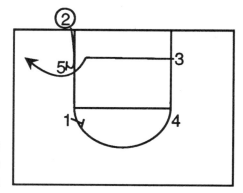

A

This play is used against a 2-3 zone defense, and is especially effective if the ball is inbounded at the halfway point between the free throw lane and the sideline. Run it with the intention of getting the ball inside.

Player #5 steps into the lane and screens the middle defender in the zone. At the same time, #3 cuts along the baseline toward the corner to draw the wing defender. After #3 cuts past #5, #5 quickly reverse pivots, putting the defender out of position.

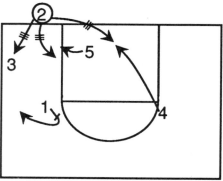

B

Player #1 screens the defensive guard on that side of the floor to maintain the two-on-two matchup in front of the ball with #3 and #5. If the defensive guard fights through the screen, #1 must step back to an open area for a pass from #2. Player #4 cuts hard from behind the zone to the baseline area, and keeps moving to find an open area to receive the ball.

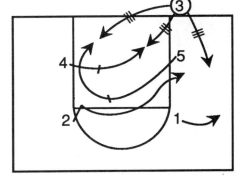

A

This is a pick-the-picker variation where #5 screens diagonally up the lane for #2, who cuts to the ball side.

Player #4 screens for #5, hoping to create a switch. If the defense does switch inside, #4 becomes the primary receiver; #1 is the safety if no scoring opportunity develops.

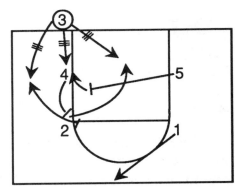

A

This is another pick-the-picker play. It is intended to force the defense to decide whether to switch or stay with their assigned players. If the defense does not communicate, the offense has the advantage.

Player #4 screens up the lane for #2, who cuts to the open area. Player #5 screens for #4; #1 is the safety. Player #4 cuts to the basket for the inbound pass. If it is not available, #5 moves toward the inbounder for a possible pass, and #2 looks for an opening on the perimeter.

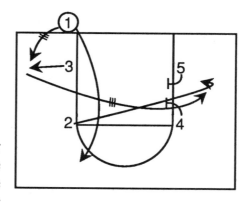

A

Player #3 steps out to the corner for the initial pass. Player #2 cuts on the weak side between #4 and #5, who have tightened up for a double screen. Player #1 inbounds, then cuts directly up the lane. Player #3 skip passes to #2 for the quick shot.

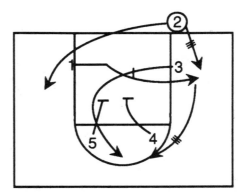

A

Player #3 screens for #1, who cuts to the ball side. Ideally, #1 receives the initial pass. After #3 screens for #1, #3 receives a double screen from #4 and #5.

After setting the screen, the big player closest to the ball turns and posts up. Player #2 empties out to the opposite side.

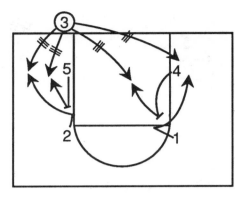

A

This is a very simple, yet dangerous, play if not defended properly.

Both big players screen up the lane. Player #2, the shooter, is on the ball side, and must wait to be screened.

If the defense switches, #5 has a mismatch in front of the ball. If #2 receives the ball on the wing and is open, a shot should be taken.

Weak-side action has #1 going to the baseline looking for an opening. Player #4 turns and finds a seam in the defense.

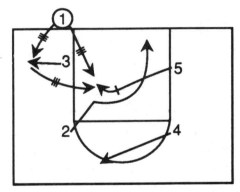

A

Player #3 steps out to the wing for the inbound pass. Player #5 cuts into the lane, and if open receives the pass from #1. If not open, #5 backscreens for #2. Player #3 can lob the ball to #2 or feed #5 in the post.

B

Player #1 empties out to the opposite side after inbounding ; #4 is the reversal player and creates a passing angle for #3 in case the ball needs to be reversed.

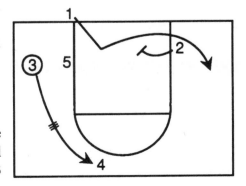

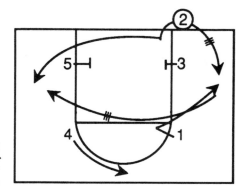

A

This play is effective against teams that trap the initial inbound pass out of a man-to-man defense or 2-3 zone defense.

Players #3 and #5 screen in as #1 cuts to the wing for the inbound pass; #2 cuts opposite the pass for a skip pass from #1 and looks for a shot. Player #4 is the safety in case the skip pass cannot be made.

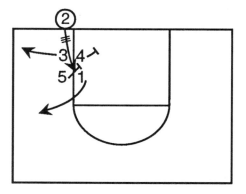

A

This is a lob play out of a rather unorthodox tight box set.

Player #3 cuts to the corner, #1 steps back as the safety, and #4 screens in as #5 steps in behind #4's screen.

Player #4 needs to step toward the basket, and the inbound pass should be thrown high and into the lane to #5.

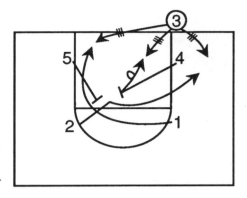

A

Players #1 and #2 cross off of #4's and #5's screens. The ball-side screener (#4) turns back for a possible lob pass. If #1's and #2's defenders switch on the cross out the next time this play is run, have #4 screen #1's defender as #1 takes the defender into the middle of the lane. This eliminates the defensive switch and frees #2 coming toward the ball.

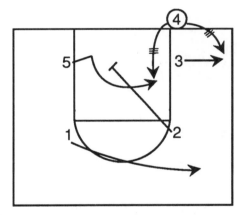

A

Player #3 steps to the corner as #2 screens diagonally down the lane for #5 at the block. Again, this forces a mismatch. If the defense switches, #5 receives the inbound pass with a smaller perimeter player as the defender.

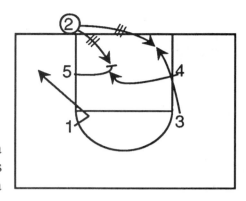

A

This play is used primarily against a zone defense. Player #5 turns and rolls behind the defensive center to set a screen.

Player #4 cuts behind #5 and uses #5 as a screen to receive a lob pass from the inbounder. At the same time, #3 cuts to the hoop to occupy the area #4 vacated for a quick pass. Player #1 is the safety.

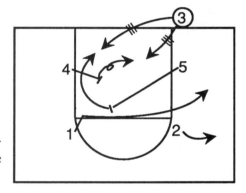

A

This is one of the countless pick-the-picker plays that is effective if the defense does not communicate on the screens.

Player #5 screens diagonally in the middle of the lane for #1. Player #4 turns and screens #5's defender. Player #5 loops around to the basket, while #4 reverse pivots to the basket if the defenders switch.

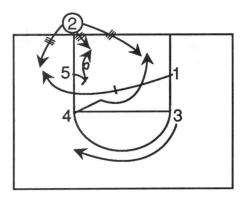

A

This is a pick-the-picker play where #1 diagonally screens for #4. The object is to force a switch defensively, which creates a mismatch inside with #1's defender guarding #4 inside.

Player #5 then screens for #1 and turns back to the ball for a possible inbound pass. Player #3 is the safety.

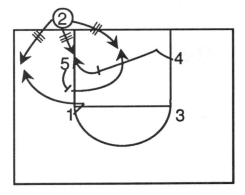

A

This pick-the-picker variation is the same as the previous play, except the personnel is moved.

Player #5 screens up the lane for #1, and #4 screens for #5. Both #4 and #5 turn to look for the pass. These pick-the-picker plays are effective because they force the defense to either stay with their players or switch to deny the pass to the cutter.

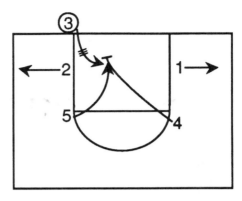

A

This is a lob play to be used against a zone defense.

Players #1 and #2 pop to the corners while #4 cuts down the middle of the lane to screen the defender for the lob pass.

Player #5, in turn, follows #4 and cuts behind, using #4 as a screen for a lob pass from the inbounder.

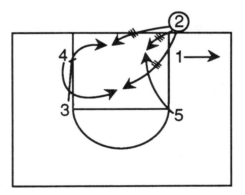

A

This is a good last-second play against a man-to-man defense. It is especially effective for teams with a big center.

Player #1 cuts to the corner, while #5 cuts up the middle of the lane looking for a lob pass from #2. Player #3 screens down for #4, who curls away from the block and finds an open area for a pass. Player #3 screens, then aggressively steps to the ball for a shot in the lane.

Stack Sets

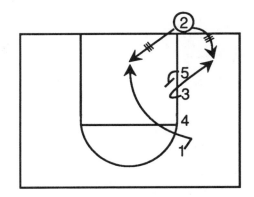

A

Player #1 sets up the defender toward the wing, then cuts toward the basket for a quick inbound pass.

Player #3 cuts to the wing; #5 looks for a lob pass; #4 is a safety outlet.

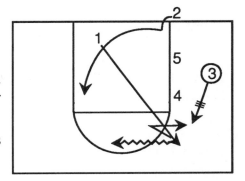

B

Player# 1, if not open for a shot inside the lane, cuts back to the top of the key for a reverse pass from #3.

C

Player #3 reverses the ball to #1, then goes down to screen for #2 at the block. On the other side, both #4 and #5 set staggered screens for #2 to come out either way.

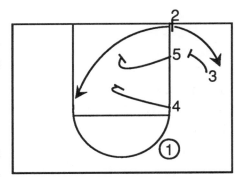

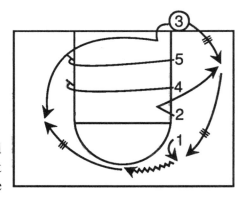

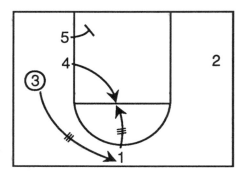

A

Player #2 fakes into the lane and pops to the wing for the inbound pass. At the same time, both #4 and #5 cross the lane to set a double screen for the inbound passer.

Player #1 steps back for ball reversal, while #3 cuts under the stack for a possible jump shot.

B

Player #4 flashes to the ball after #3 reverses the ball back to #1.

Player #5 steps hard to the basket and looks to seal the defender for a possible lob from #1.

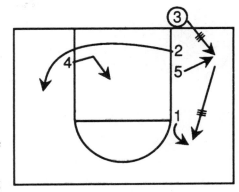

A

Player #5 cuts to the corner to receive the inbound pass.

Player #2 cuts underneath #4, and #5 reverses the ball to #1. As #1 catches the ball, #4 tries to seal the defender for a possible post feed.

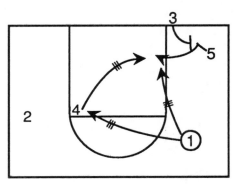

B

Player #3 steps out to screen for #5 after #5 reverses the ball to #1. Player #4 also can pass to #5 after #5 comes off of #3's screen.

Option: If #5's defender does not come out to contest on the perimeter, #5 can screen in for #3.

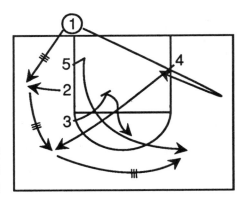

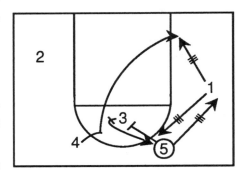

A

Player #2 steps out to the wing for the inbound pass. Player #3 screens for #5 as both #4 and #5 cross out to the top of the key. Player #2 passes to #4, who reverses the ball to #5. Player #1 cuts to the wing, then back cuts for the backdoor pass.

B

If #1 is not closely guarded and cannot go backdoor, #5 passes to #1 on the wing.

Player #3 then sets a screen at the free throw line for #4, who shuffle cuts to the basket.

Player #5 then screens down for #3 at the free throw line for a jump shot.

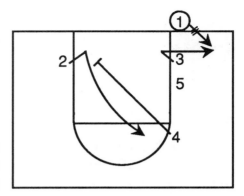

A

Player #3 cuts to the corner for the inbound pass. As #3 is receiving the pass on the wing, #4 screens down for #2 at the opposite block.

Player #3 looks first to #4, who is stepping toward the ball after screening down. Player #3 then looks to #2 coming off the pick for the jump shot.

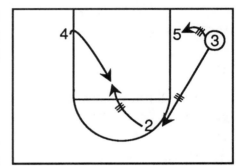

B

If #3 is not open for the shot, a triangle alignment is formed and #3 can post feed #5 at the block or reverse the ball to #2. As #2 catches the ball, #4 flashes toward the free throw line. If #4 receives the pass, #4 can either shoot the ball or post feed to #5. If #5's defender is playing on the top side, #5 should slide the defender up the lane and then seal off for a lob pass.

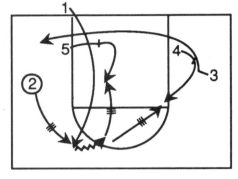

A

This play can result in a quick lob opportunity, but has other options if the lob is not available.

Players #2 and #3 flare out to the wings. Players #4 and #5 cross in the lane as they cut toward the ball. If the defense switches, a lob opportunity should be present for one of the big players.

Also, if #4's and #5's defenders back up toward the basket in the lane, #4 and #5 should screen in on #2's and #3's defenders. This gives the offense a jump shot.

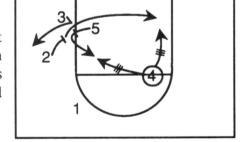

B

If #2 receives the ball but cannot shoot, #1 cuts up the lane for a return pass. After #1 catches the ball, #4 steps out to the wing to backscreen for #3 and then flashes toward the ball.

C

Player #4 can shoot if open. Player #3 back cuts, then continues through the lane and receives a screen from #2 on the wing. Player #5 then screens for #2 and turns to look for a pass from #4.

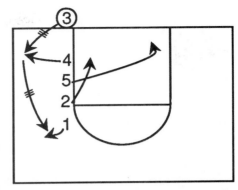

A

This play in intended for the perimeter jump shooters.

Player #4 cuts hard to the corner to receive the inbound pass. Player #5 cuts to the opposite block, #2 cuts to the block in front of the ball and #1 is the safety. Player #4 reverses the ball to #1 out on the perimeter.

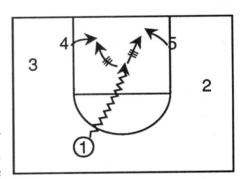

B

Player #1 has the option of passing to either #3 or #2 for the jump shot. After #4 and #5 have screened, they immediately turn to look for the ball.

C

This low set also affords an opportunity for #1 to take the ball and penetrate into the lane, in which case if either #4's or #5's defenders step into the lane, #1 can dump a pass to either of these players.

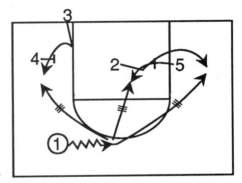

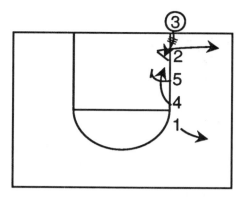

A

Player #2 cuts to the corner as #5 steps into the lane and, like a blocker in football, leads "interference" for #4. Player #4 steps in directly behind #5 looking for the lob pass. Player #1 is the safety.

B

If the ball is inbounded to #2, and #2 reverses it to #1, #5 screens for the inbounder in the lane. Player #3 can make a curl cut around #5 in the lane or can cut to the free throw line looking for a pass from #1. Player #2 also can screen in for #3 on the wing.

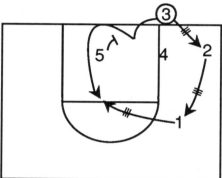

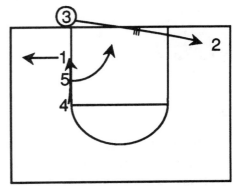

A

This is a stack set with your best shooter in the far corner.

Player #1 cuts hard to the corner while #5 steps into the lane in front of the basket to seal the defender and look for a short lob or bounce pass.

Player #4 cuts directly up the lane looking for the inbound pass. Player #2 is in the opposite corner even with the backboard so the inbounder can pass underneath the defense. Player #2 has the green light to shoot the ball immediately.

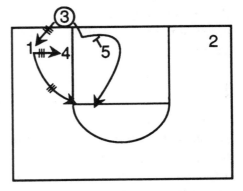

B

If #1 receives the inbound pass, #4 looks to post up. Player #5 screens for #3, who cuts through the lane toward the top of the key.

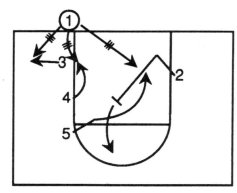

A

Player #3 cuts to the corner. Player #4 stays still until #2 has screened for #5, then #4 cuts down the lane toward the ball.

B

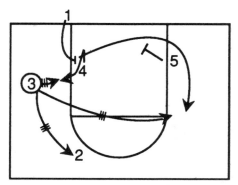

If #4 and #5 are not open for the inbound pass, #3 receives the pass from #1. Player #1 screens for #4 in the middle of the lane, then cuts to the weak side. Player #3 can post feed #4, can reverse the ball to #2 or can skip pass to #1, who has cut to the weak side.

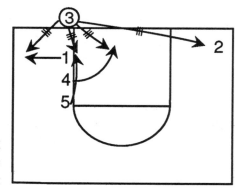

A

Players #1, #4 and #5 line up along the free throw lane. Player #2 is in the opposite corner positioned even (or just below) the backboard along the baseline.

Player #1 cuts to the baseline corner and #4 steps into the lane, right in front of the basket. Player #5 cuts up the middle of the lane looking for the ball. The inbounder has four passing options. If #1 receives the inbound pass, #1 can engage in a two-player game with #5, who is posting up.

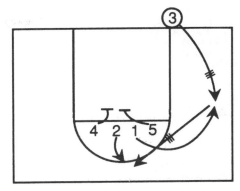

A

This play is designed to result in a quick three-pointer.

Player #1 loops out of the straight line to receive the inbound pass. At the same time, #4 and #5 close the gap and screen #2's defender. Player #2 steps back for the shot.

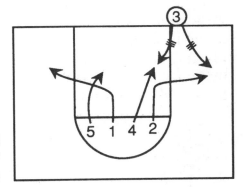

A

The objective of this play is to bring the defense up the lane and then away from the basket, clearing space for a short jumper.

Players #1 and #2 cut to the corners and #4 and #5 cut down the lane. Ideally, the first pass is made into the lane for a short shot.

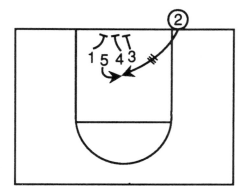

A

The players line up across the lane in front of the basket. Player #5 curls around the line of screeners for a lob pass.

Usually, the defense will have its big players between the basket and the offense, and its smaller players behind the straight line. The center must be able to out-jump a guard.

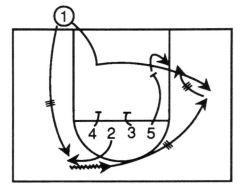

A

The offense lines up at the free throw line. Player #2 cuts to receive the inbound pass as #3 and #4 screen in.

Player #5 cuts down the lane to screen the inbounder. Player #2 passes the ball to #1 for a shot, or #1 can post feed to #5 at the block.

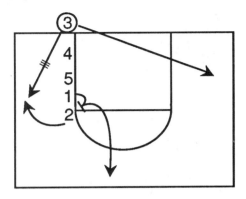

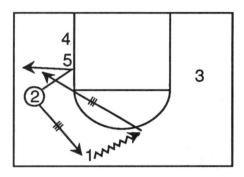

A

This play can result in a quick three-pointer.

Player #1 sets a screen for #2, who fakes toward the lane and pops out to the wing to receive the inbound pass. Player #1 steps out near the top of the key.

B

If #2 is not open for a shot off of the inbound pass, the pass is made to #1, who takes a couple of dribbles away from the play. Player #2 then cuts toward #4 and #5, who remain stationary, and tries to rub the defender off of them. Player #2 then cuts back to the three-point line for a pass from #1 and a possible shot.

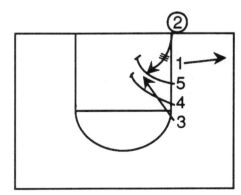

A

This is another play that is used primarily against a zone defense.

Player #1 cuts to the corner while #4 and #5 set a double screen for #3 for a lob pass. Player #3 must come in behind #4 and #5 as they lead "interference" in the middle of the lane for #3.

Diamond Sets

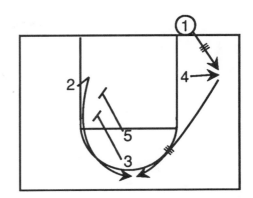

A

Many effective options are available out of this alignment.

Player #4 cuts to the corner for the initial pass, while #3 and #5 set a double screen for #2 for the jump shot.

If the defense switches, one of the screeners (#3 or #5) must come back to the ball.

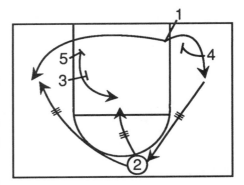

B

Option: Player #4 steps out for the inbound pass and reverses the ball to #2. Players #5 and #3 double screen for the inbounder. Player #2 can pass to #1 for a jumper, or pass to #5, who curls around #3 looking for a pass in the lane.

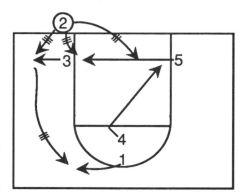

A

Player #3 cuts hard to the corner as #5 cuts to the ball-side block. Player #4 sets up the defender and cuts to the weak-side block; #1 is the safety.

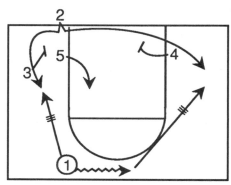

B

If #5 and #4 are not open after their intial cuts, the ball is inbounded to #1. Player #5 then posts up looking for an interior pass. The inbounder, #2, can empty out on either side for a return pass from #1.

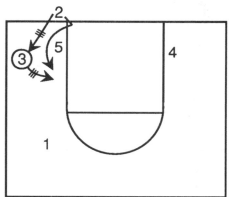

C

Option: Have #2 pass the ball to the corner. Player #5 has cut across the lane, and after #3 has received the ball, #5 turns and screens #2's defender in the lane. Player #2 then curls around #5 looking for a quick return pass from #3.

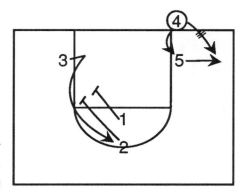

A

Player #5 steps out to the corner for the inbound pass as both #1 and #2 double screen for #3, who is looking for the jump shot. Player #4 steps inbounds to post up after #5 receives the ball.

B

Player #5 has two passing options — to #4 posting up or to #3 on the perimeter.

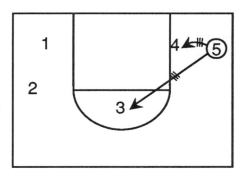

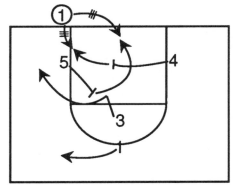

A

Player #5 turns to screen up the lane for #3, who cuts to the ball. Player #4 cuts across the lane to screen #5's defender. If #4's defender helps on #5's cut, #4 reverse pivots and seals #5's defender in the lane for the inbound pass from #1.

64

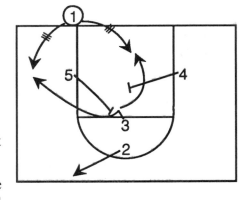

A

This play can result in a quick basket for a post player if executed properly.

Player #5 picks for #3 at the free throw line, #4 picks the picker and screens for #5; #2 is the safety.

Player #5 rolls to the basket looking for the inbound pass. If that is not open, the second option is to look for #3 on the perimeter.

65

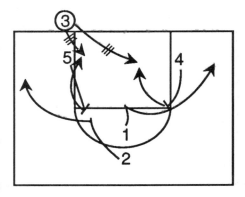

A

This play also can free a post player rolling toward the basket.

Players #4 and #5 each screen up the lane for a perimeter cutter. Player #5 then rolls back to the ball, while #4 steps toward the front of the basket.

Baseline Sets

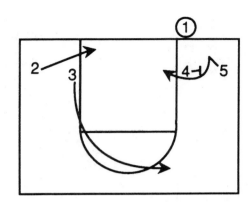

A

The ball is designed to come to the inbounder, so the primary perimeter shooter should take the ball out of bounds.

Player #4 screens for #5, who cuts to the hoop. Player #3 flashes to the ball-side wing and #2 cuts hard into the lane looking for a pass.

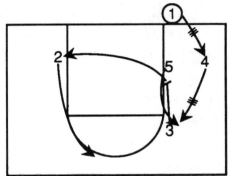

B

Player #1 passes to #4 in the corner while #3 screens down for #5 and then clears out. Player #2 empties out to the top of the key.

Option: If #3's defender switches onto #5, #5 dives to the ball-side block to take advantage of the mismatch.

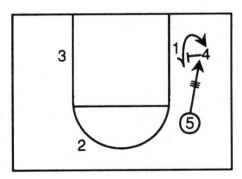

C

Player #4 screens in for #1 for a jump shot and #4 turns to post up on the block.

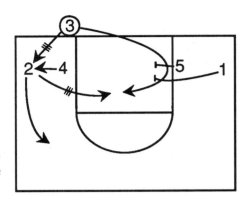

A

Player #2 clears out of the corner and #4 cuts hard to receive the pass from the inbounder.

Player #3 clears out on the opposite side or makes a curl cut back into the lane.

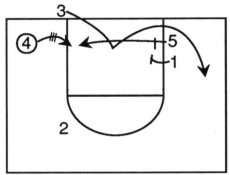

B

Option: Player #4 can feed #5, who cuts across the lane and posts up inside.

C

Option: Player #4 can pass to #2, who passes to #1, who has cut to the perimeter. Player #3 must read the defense and either curl into the lane or cut out to the wing.

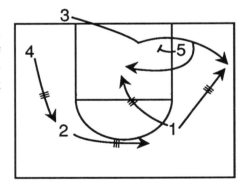

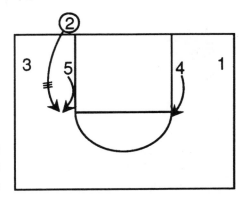

A

Player #5 rolls back toward the free throw line for the inbound pass. As the pass is made, #4 cuts hard up the lane to the other side of the free throw line.

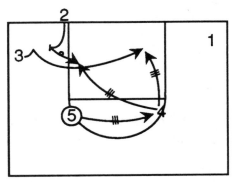

B

Player #5 reverses the ball to #4. Meanwhile, #2 steps in and backscreens #3's defender. Player #2 screens, then steps toward the ball. Player #4 can pass to either #2 or #3.

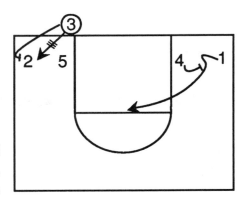

A

Player #3 passes to #2 and follows the pass behind #2 for a return handoff. Player #2 hands the ball off for #3 for a quick jump shot.

On the weak side, #4 turns and screens for #1, who sets up the defender toward the baseline and then cuts back into the lane.

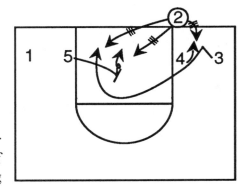

A

Player #5 sets a diagonal screen for #3, then turns to look for the lob pass. If #3's defender attempts to beat #3 along the baseline, #4 should screen #3's defender. Otherwise, #4 seals the defender and look for a short inbound pass.

Random Sets

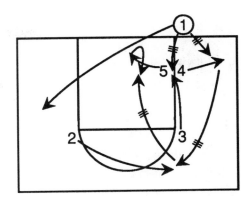

A

Players #4 and #5 start shoulder to shoulder at the block. Player #4 cuts to the corner, #5 posts up in lane and #3 cuts up the lane for a quick inbound pass. Player #2 is the safety.

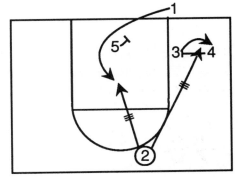

B

If the ball is inbounded and reversed to #2, #5 screens for #1 for a curl cut in the lane and #4 screens in for #3.

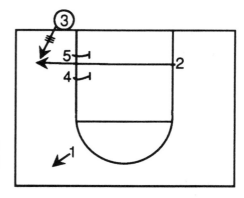

A

Player #2 cuts between the double screen set by #4 and #5 for the inbound pass; #1 is the safety.

B

If #2 does not shoot the ball, #2 reverses it to #1 and receives a backscreen from #5. Player #4 screens for the inbounder and then flashes toward the ball up the lane. Player #1 has three passing options — to #2 cutting into the lane or to #3 or #4 cutting toward the perimeter.

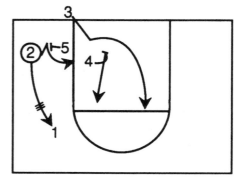

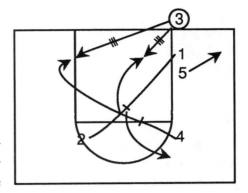

A

Player #1 sets a diagonal screen for #2 as #5 steps out to the corner. Player #4 screens for #1, then cuts hard to the opposite block looking for the ball.

B

If #2 and #4 are not open and the ball is inbounded to #5, #5 reverses the ball to #1, while #2 screens for the inbounder, #3. Player #3 also receives a baseline screen from #5 and can cut either way to look for a pass.

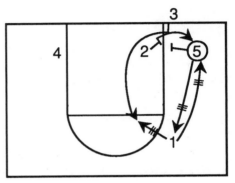

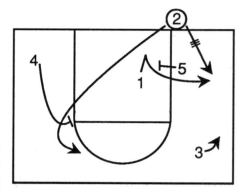

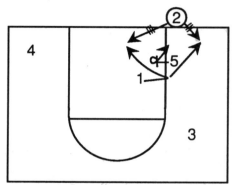

A

Player #5 steps into the lane to screen for #1, who sets up the defender by faking toward the baseline and then cutting off of the pick to receive the inbound pass. Player #4 sets up wide and has the option of screening for #2 at the elbow. Player #1 looks for the shot or engages #5 in a two-player game.

B

Option: Player #1 must read the defense by cutting off of #5's screen in the opposite direction of the defender. If #5's defender switches to #1, #5 quickly pivots toward the ball and looks for the inbound pass.

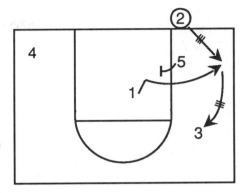

A

The same play also can be run to free the inbounder.

Player #5 screens for #1, and #1 passes to #3 after receiving the inbound pass.

B

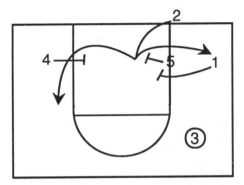

Player #4 screens in on the weak side while #1 and #5 screen in on the ball side; #2 can go either way to look for a pass from #3. .

Option: If #1's defender switches onto #2 off of the double screen, then #1 should cut underneath #4 on the weak side. Player #1 should be open.

C

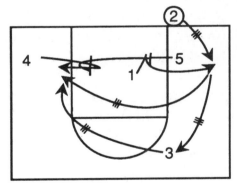

Option: Player #5 screens for #1, who cuts to the corner to receive the inbound pass. Player #5 then continues across the lane to screen for #4. If #4's defender cheats and gets caught in the lane, #5 should screen again on #4's defender. Player #4 then flares back for a skip pass from #1.

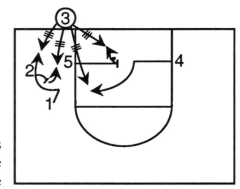

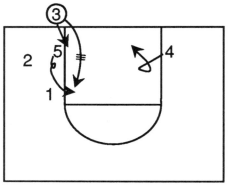

A

This is a series of plays that requires players to read the defense. The objective is to clear the defensive help out of the lane, thus giving the post players room to maneuver.

Player #5 screens across for #4; #4 looks for a lob pass. Player #5 turns back to the ball after setting the screen. Player #2 screens for #1, then #1 cuts to the corner for a potential shot. If the defense switches, #2 pivots and comes toward the ball.

B

Option: Player #5 rolls back up the lane looking to seal the defender on the baseline side. The inbounder lobs the ball to #5 and then quickly steps in for an instantaneous return pass (a touch pass in the air right back to the in-bounder). On the weak-side block, #4 fakes high and then reverse pivots and steps low to pin the defender in the lane for a bounce pass from the inbounder.

Again, #2 screens for #1. If the defense switches and #2's defender takes #1 coming off the screen, #2 pivots and comes directly to the ball.

C

Option: Similar alignment, but #5 cuts to the corner as #1 diagonally down-screens for #4. Player #4 cuts around the screen for a possible lob; #2 stays wide as the safety. If the ball is inbounded to #5 in the corner, #3 immediately steps in and aggressively posts up at the block for a return pass from #5.

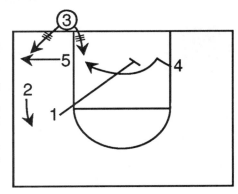

D

Option: Player #5 cuts to the corner while #4 rolls in an attempt to pin the defender for a baseline bounce pass. Player #2 cuts directly to the ball and is very physical in establishing position for a short lob pass or bounce pass.

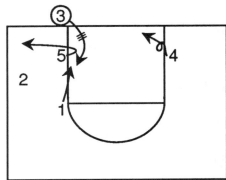

E

Option: If #5's defender does not line up between the ball and the assigned player, #3 makes a quick low bounce pass to #5 and immediately steps into the lane to rebound for #5, who is instructed to catch and shoot it.

If #1's defender is sagging, #2 back-screens #1's defender.

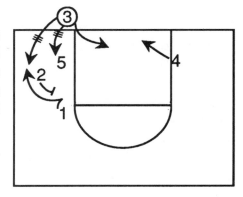

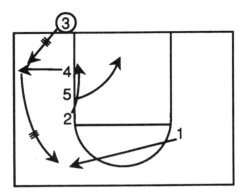

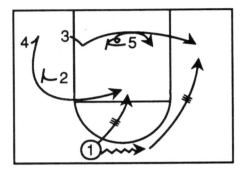

A

Player #4 cuts to the corner to receive the inbound pass. Player #5 cuts to the front of the hoop and tries to seal the defender for a pass from the inbounder. If the pass is not available, #5 steps to the opposite block. Player #2 cuts directly up the lane looking for a dump pass, but if the pass is not available, #2 should step back up the lane in order to allow #3 to post up after #3 inbounds the ball.

B

Player #4, after receiving the inbound pass, reverses it to #1, who takes it on the dribble to the other side of the floor. At the same time, #5 screens along the baseline for #3, who cuts to the wing. Player #5 then reverse pivots and comes to the ball side looking for a pass. Player #2 screens for #4, who makes a curl cut looking for a pass in the lane.

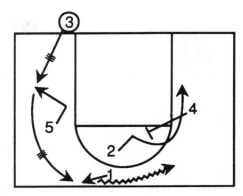

A

This play uses the backscreen lob pass as an option to score.

Player #5 cuts to receive the inbound pass, and #1 steps back to get open for ball reversal. As #1 is dribbling toward the top of the circle, #4 looks for #2's defender to backscreen.

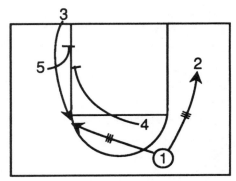

B

Player #1 takes the ball toward the backscreen set by #4 for #2. Player #5 then looks to screen for #3. Player #4 screens for #3, who looks for a possible jump shot at the free throw line.

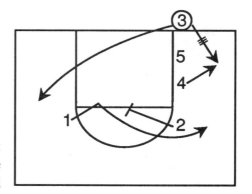

A

Players #4 and #5 line up in a stack in front of the ball. Player #4 cuts to the corner for the inbound pass. Player #2 can screen for #1, or #2 can just cut and replace to receive the pass from #4. Player #3 empties out to the weak side

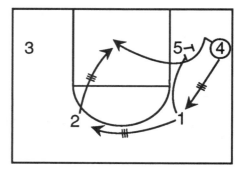

B

The ball is reversed to #2 through #1. Players #5 and #1 then set a double screen for #4, who makes a curl cut into the lane.

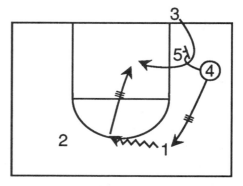

C

Option: Instead of the inbound passer cutting to the weak side as in Diagram A, both #4 and #5 can turn and screen for #3 after the ball is reversed. Here #3 can either curl or flare to the corner if the defender cheats underneath the screen.

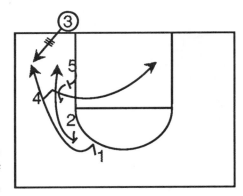

A

Player #5 turns and screens for #4, who cuts into the lane looking for the inbound pass. Player #2 screens for #1, who cuts to the wing as #5 screens for #2, who cuts to the basket looking for a layup or short jump shot.

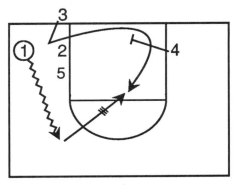

B

Player #1 receives the inbound pass and takes the ball on the dribble toward the top of the key. Player #3 fakes toward the ball side. This sets up the defender as #4 screens in for the inbounder. Player #3 looks for a shot in the lane on a tight curl cut if the defender follows.

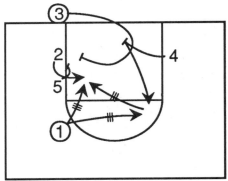

C

Option: Player #4 screens, then pops back to the free throw line for a pass from #1. If #3 does not catch the ball off of the curl, #3 and #5 set a double screen for #2, who makes another curl move into the lane.

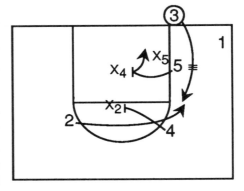

A

Player #5 starts at the midpost, then turns and screens for #4. Player #4 cuts toward the hoop either way off of #5's screen. If #4's defender takes the fake to the outside, #4 can cut up the middle of the lane. If #5's defender switches to #4 on #4's cut, #5 must immediately turn and look for the ball.

Player #2 cuts right behind #4 and heads to the wing. Player #1 is in the ball-side corner. If #1's defender helps on #4's cut to the basket, the ball should be passed to #1 for the shot. Player #5 screens for #2, then turns and looks for a pass from the inbounder.

B

Option: If #4's defender stays in the lane and does not cover #4 on the perimeter, #5 screens #4's defender and then quickly reverse pivots for the inbound pass in the lane, while #4 screens #2's defender as #2 cuts to the ball side.

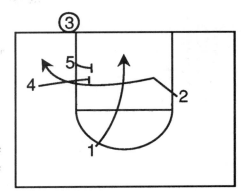

A

Player #2 cuts off of the double screen by #4 and #5. Player #1 cuts to the hoop right off of #2's cut.

B

If #2 catches but cannot score, #4 and #5 double screen for the inbounder. Player #1 stays wide on the weak side spreading out the defense.

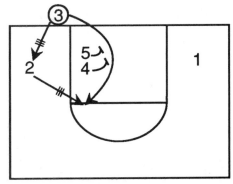

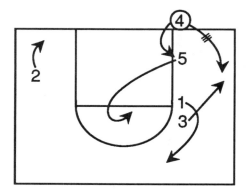

A

Player #3 cuts to the wing for the inbound pass, while #1 cuts to the top as a safety. Player #5 steps back to the free throw line. The inbounder passes to the corner and steps in for a quick return pass.

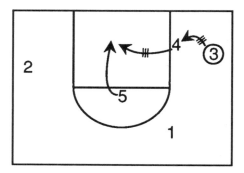

B

If #3 passes to #4, #5 immediately cuts to the basket for a quick dump pass. (This works especially well when #5's defender goes down to double team #4 in the low post.)

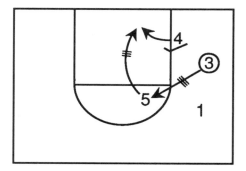

C

Player #3 tries to post feed #4. If #4 is fronted, #3 passes to #5, who looks for a lob pass to #4 as #4 seals the defender at the block.

D

Option: If #5 cannot pass the ball to #4, #5 reverses the ball to #2 and cuts down the lane. This pass keys #3 and #4 to backscreen #1's defender for a skip pass from #2. (This backscreen eliminates the weak-side help on #5.)

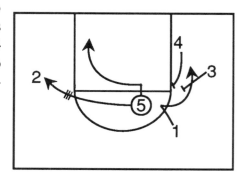

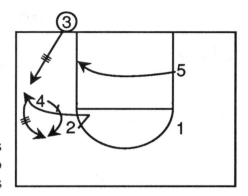

A

Player #4 screens for #2 as #5 flashes hard across the lane for a possible lob from the inbounder. Player #2 receives the inbound pass and reverses it to #4.

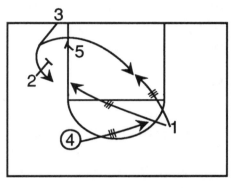

B

Player #4 reverses the ball to #1. The inbounder, #3, has the option of coming out either side, either accepting #2's screen or cutting underneath #5 for a post-up in the lane. This play is especially effective for an inbounder who can maneuver inside.

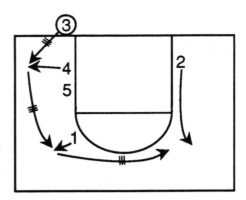

A

Player #4 steps out to the corner for the inbounder. Player #5 then looks for a pass from #4, while #1 steps outs for a reversal pass from #4.

Player #2 steps out to catch from #1. This ball reversal should be made as quickly as possible.

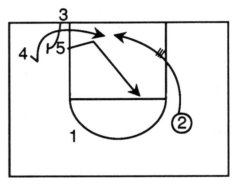

B

After #2 catches the ball, #5 cuts hard to the ball. The inbounder then steps in to backscreen for #4 for a lob pass or a post feed on the block by #2.

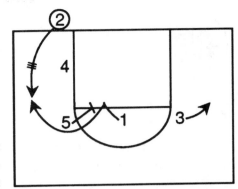

A

Players #5, #1 and #3 form a straight line along the free throw line. Player #4 posts on the block. Player #1 takes the defender down into the lane to set up the defender and then cuts off of #5's screen to the wing for the inbound pass.

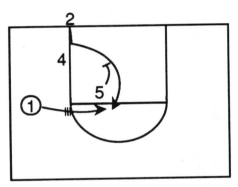

B

Player #2 then cuts off of #5 up the middle of the lane for a potential jump shot.

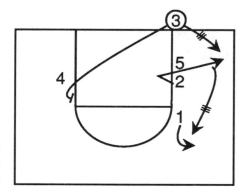

A

Player #2 cuts to the corner for the inbound pass and #1 steps back for the reversal pass. Player #3 stacks up with #4 after the inbound pass is made. As an option, #3 can take the defender into the lane; if the defender cheats, #3 can come right back out under #5 for a short jump shot on the baseline.

B

Player #1 has the ball; the passing options include taking the ball to the other side of the floor and passing to #2, who runs underneath screens set by both #5 and #4. At the same time, #3 steps quickly into the lane for a pass in the lane. Player #1 also can reverse the dribble back to #5 for a post feed.

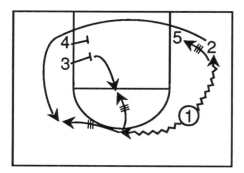

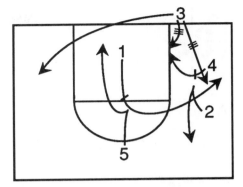

A

This play is to be used against an aggressive man-to-man defense.

Player #1 screens up for #5, who cuts to the basket looking for a lob or bounce pass.

Players #4 and #2 screen in for #1, then #4 steps to the basket and #2 becomes the safety. The inbounder empties to the opposite side.

B

Option: Player #4 screens #2's defender and then pops to the corner for a possible shot. Player #4 steps to the ball and #1 becomes the safety.

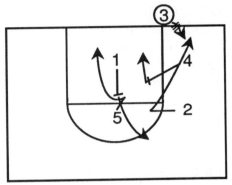

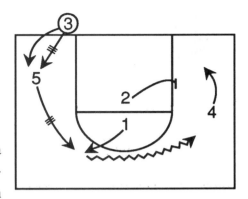

A

This play is designed to create a post-up situation for a perimeter player.

Players #4 and #5 stay wide; #3 can inbound to #5 or pass directly to #1. Player #2 posts up in the lane.

B

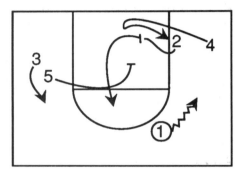

Player #5 reverses the ball to #1, who takes it on the dribble toward #4. Player #4 empties out on the wing as the ball is dribbled that direction . Player #5 flashes to the free throw line. After #4 gets under the basket, #2 turns and screens for #4, who comes back to the ball-side block. Player #5 then screens down the lane for #2, who cuts hard to the free throw line and looks for a shot.

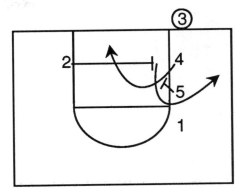

A

This is another variation of a pick-the-picker play.

Player #2 screens for #4, and #4 looks for a quick inbound pass. Player #5 quickly screens for #2 for the jump shot — this will be open.

If #2 and #5's defenders switch, a guard is defending a center standing on the ball-side block.

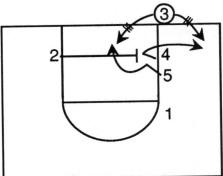

B

Option: Player #4 steps into the lane if the defender cheats to avoid the screen from #2. Player #4 then cuts out to the wing to receive the inbound pass.

If #4 does not shoot the ball, #2 screens #5's defender and #5 loops around to the front of the basket for a possible lob pass from #4.

A

Player #5 screens in the middle of the lane for #3, who pops to the wing for the inbound pass.

Player #5 continues up the lane to screen for #1, who cuts to the basket for a possible lob pass. Player #4 remains still until #5 sets the initial screen on #3; #4 then cuts down the lane line for a possible lob or short bounce pass.

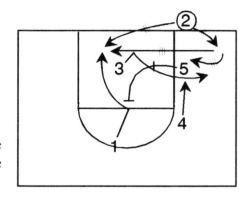

A

Player #4 turns and screens in for #1 for the inbound pass. Both #4 and #5 then screen for the inbounder for a curl move around the double screen. Player #3 screens in on the weak side, giving #2 the option of going either way after the the ball is put into play to look for a return pass.

This play also affords #1 room to penetrate into the lane because the defense is forced along the baseline.

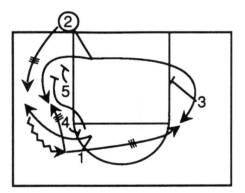

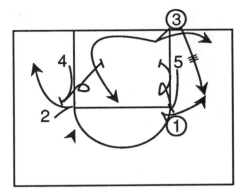

A

Players #4 and #5 step up the lane and screen for the players on the wings. After screening, #4 and #5 roll to the basket. After the ball is inbounded to the ball-side wing player, #4 and #5 look to screen for the inbounder, #3.

The player receiving the inbound pass (either #1 or #2) looks for #3 coming off of the screen, either up the lane or on the baseline. The ball also can be passed to a big player posting up inside.

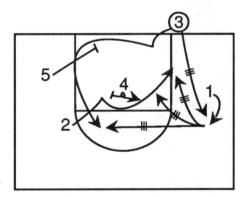

A

Player #3 inbounds to #1 on the wing. Player #4 screens for #2 in the lane, and #5 steps into the lane to screen for the inbounder if the defense switches on #4's screen for #2. A mismatch is created and #4 should reverse pivot for the pass from #1.

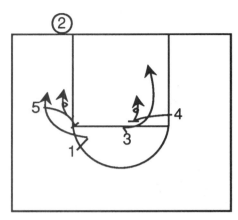

A

This play is designed to spread the defense and get the offense off of the baseline.

Both #4 and #5 screen in for #1 and #3, who read the defense and cut hard to receive the inbound pass. Both screeners turn back to the ball as secondary receivers. Four simultaneous scoring threats now are available.

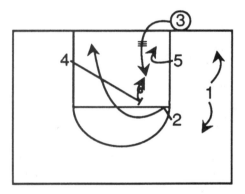

A

This play is designed primarily for use against a 1-3-1 zone defense. It is effective because of the mismatch created in the lane with a big player screening a perimeter player.

Player #1 cuts to an open area and is primarily a safety. Player #5 is posting up looking for a short bounce pass for a power move, while #4 screens on the defender guarding #2 (this usually is a guard). Player #4 then reverse pivots and looks for the ball from the inbounder.

Side Outs

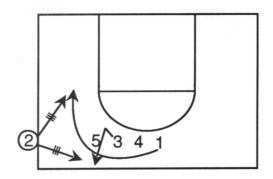

A

The players form a straight line for a three-point attempt. Player #1 cuts around the top of the stack, and if open because the defender trails, immediately receives the inbound pass for the shot. Player #3 then steps back (after #1 has made the cut) for the inbound pass.

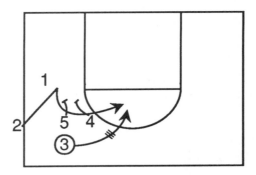

B

Player #2 then steps inbounds and takes the defender toward the basket. Player #2 uses #4 and #5 as screeners to get a return pass from #3 for a potential three-point shot.

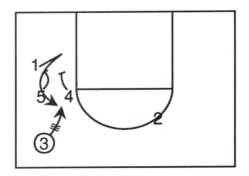

C

If #2 is not in a position to catch and shoot, #4 and #5 continue down to screen for #1, who cuts over the double screen for a possible jump shot.

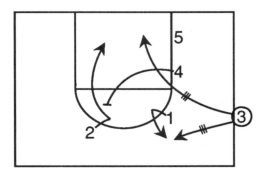

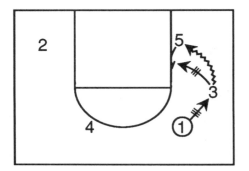

A

Player #1 cuts to receive the inbound pass. Player #4 loops toward the top of the key as #2 sets up the defender by stepping toward the ball as if to receive the pass. Player #4 then backscreens #2's defender. If open, #2 receives the lob pass from #3. Player #5 slides up the lane to draw the defender away from the basket.

B

If the lob cannot be thrown and the inbound pass is made to #1 instead, #1 returns the ball to the inbounder, #3, who can either post feed #5 or take the ball one-on-one toward the baseline and try to score.

If #5's defender is on the high side, #5 should slide the defender up the lane a few feet in order to give #3 an opportunity to drive baseline.

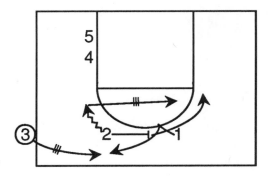

A

Player #2 screens away to get #1 open for the inbound pass. Player #1 catches and reverses the ball to #2 (or #1 can take the ball on the dribble and #2 must clear out). Players #4 and #5 are in a stack set on the ball side.

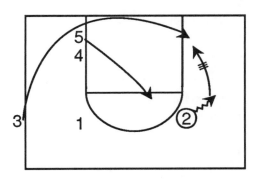

B

Player #2 takes the ball on the dribble as #3 cuts underneath the stack for either a post up or a short jump shot. Player #5 flashes to the free throw line right after #3 cuts underneath.

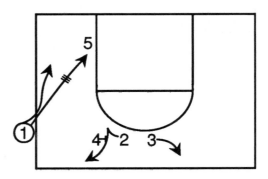

A

This is an isolation for the post player at the block. A stack set is formed in front of the ball. It is most effective when the defense needs to guard everyone — which probably would be late in the half or the game.

Player #4 turns and screens for #2, who cuts to the ball and is a safety outlet. Player #3 creates space by flaring out to the opposite side.

B

Player #1 throws to #5 and follows the pass for a jump shot. Remember, the player throwing the ball into play often is the most dangerous scoring threat.

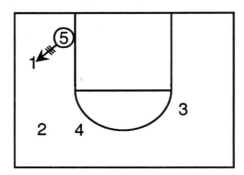

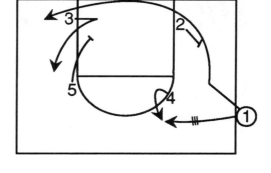

A

Player #4 cuts and replaces in order to get free for the inbound pass. Player #5 screens for #3 as #1 cuts underneath both #2 and #5.

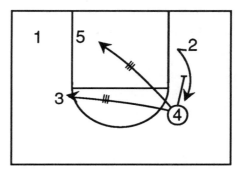

B

Player #4 can reverse the ball to #3 for a jump shot, or #4 can make a direct passes to #5 in the lane. If #4 passes to #3, #1 stays wide in order to isolate #5 inside. Player #4, after passing to #3, screens down for #2 for a jump shot. This screen also helps to occupy the weak-side defense.

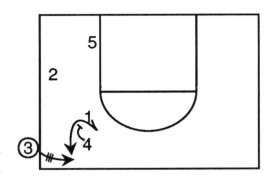

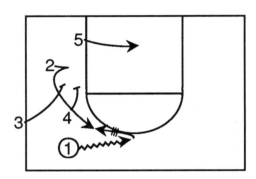

A

This play is designed to free a jump shooter and to isolate a post player. Because the alignment spreads the defense out on the floor, it is a rather safe play to run to inbound the ball.

Player #4 screens for #1, who receives the inbound pass.

B

Player #1 dribbles to the middle of the floor, and takes the defender one-on-one if possible. Players #4 and #3 set staggered screens for #2 for the potential score.

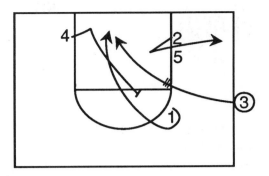

A

Player #2 ducks into the lane and uses #5 as a screener to get free for a jump shot along the baseline. At the same time, #4 backscreens for #1 for the lob pass to the basket.

B

If the lob opportunity does not present itself, #3 passes the ball to #4. Player #4 immediately looks inside to #5 for a high/low pass. The lane is cleared out for #5 to go from one side of the lane to the other.

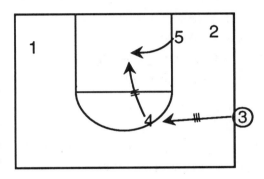

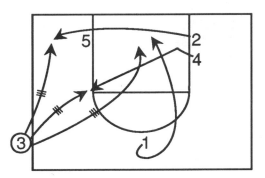

A

This alignment is similar to the one shown in the previous diagram. Player #2 runs underneath #5 for a possible pass along the baseline. Player #4 flashes to the elbow; if #4 catches, the first option is to look inside to #5. As #4 is flashing toward the ball, #1 sets up the defender by stepping toward midcourt, then quickly reverse pivots and cuts hard to the basket for a lob pass.

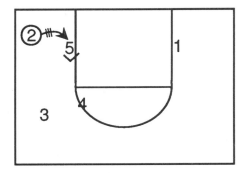

B

If #2 catches the ball in the corner, the defender guarding #5 is usually caught defending #5 on the high side. This is an excellent opportunity for a baseline pass into the post.

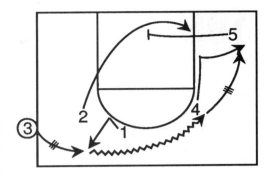

A

Players #1 and #2 line up in front of the inbounder. Player #1 cuts to get the ball and then dribbles at #4, who makes a sharp cut to the corner. At the same time, #5 is screening in the lane for #2, who is going to post up.

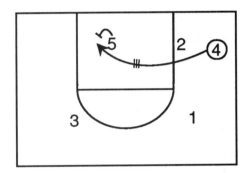

B

Player #4 receives the pass from #1 and looks for the lob pass to #5. This should be available because #5's defender will be playing between the ball and #5. Player #5 pins the defender in the lane and #4 throws the ball.

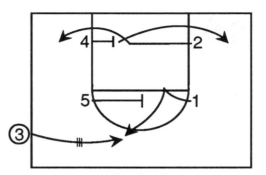

A

Players #4 and #5 both screen across the lane. Player #1 comes to receive the inbound pass from #3. Player #2 cuts toward the corner trying to get open for the jump shot. Player #4 continues to the opposite corner to wait for the ball.

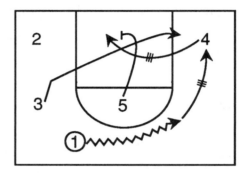

B

Player #5 screens for #1, and rolls back into the lane and screens for #3, who cuts hard to post up for the ball. Player #5 then turns and seals the defender and looks for the lob pass from #4. Again, the defender probably will be playing between the ball and #5, which creates the lob opportunity.

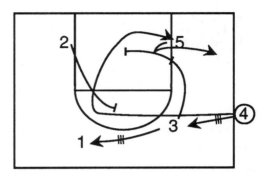

A

Player #4 inbounds the ball to #3, who passes to #1. Player #3 then goes to the block to screen for #5, who cuts to the corner. Player #2 flashes from the opposite block and screens for #4, who curls around #2's screen. Player #3 continues into the lane to screen for #4.

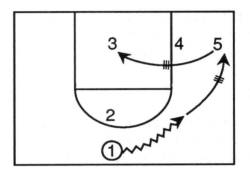

B

Player #1 passes to #5 in the corner. Player #5's first look is to #3 in the lane on a lob pass over the top. Player #3's defender probably will be between #3 and the ball, so #3 can seal off the defender and show a target hand to the passer in the corner.

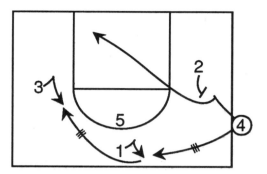

A

Player #1 cuts to get open to receive the inbound pass, then reverses the ball to #3. Player #2 sets a "headhunting" screen for #4 for a baseline cut through the lane. If #4 is open, a layup results.

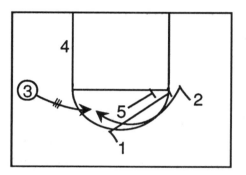

B

If #4 is unable to receive the pass, both #1 and #5 set a double screen for #2, who is looking for the jump shot. Player #5 comes back to the ball after screening.

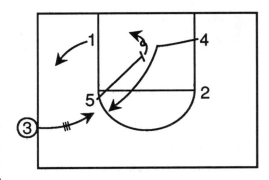

A

Player #5 screens for #4. Player #1 cuts hard to the ball from the ball-side block as a secondary receiver and #4 catches the inbound pass. If #5's defender switches on to #4 as #4 comes to the ball, #5 pivots and seals in the lane, looking for a pass from #3.

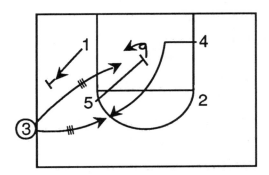

B

After #4 has caught the inbound pass from #3, #1 steps up and back-screens for the inbounder for a cut to the basket. Player #3 continues through the lane and receives a double screen from #2 and #5.

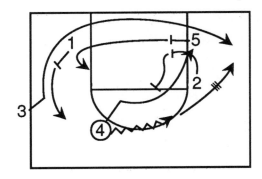

C

Player #4 reverses the ball to #3, then receives a backscreen from #2. Player #2 then steps to the perimeter and #5 comes to the free throw line to empty out the baseline. If #5's defender helps on #4's basket cut, #5 is open to catch the ball and shoot. If #5's defender goes with #5 to the free throw line, #4 should be able to receive a pass and score.

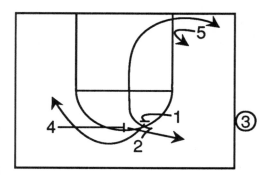

A

This is an effective play for end-of-game situations.

Player #5 is on the baseline and moves to the block to post up for the ball. At the same time, #2 receives a screen beyond the top of the circle from #1 while cutting down the middle. Player #2 cuts underneath #5 to the corner.

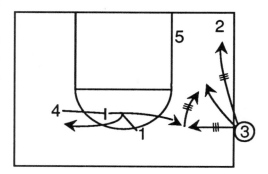

B

Player #4 screens for #1, who fades to the opposite wing for a potential lob pass. Player #4 then steps to the ball as a safety. Player #3 inbounds the ball, then steps in to spot up along the three-point line for a return pass. (Many times the most dangerous threat to score is the inbound passer who receives a quick return pass for an open shot.)

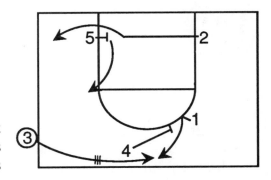

A

Player #4 screens away for #1 out in front of the ball. Player #5 screens for #2 along the baseline, then turns and comes up the lane.

B

Player #1 receives the inbound pass, then reverses the ball to #4. Player #5 then screens for #3 on a diagonal cut through the lane to the basket. After #3's cut has been made, both #1 and #5 turn and screen for #2, who is coming off of the double screen for the jump shot.

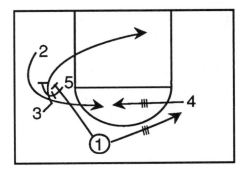

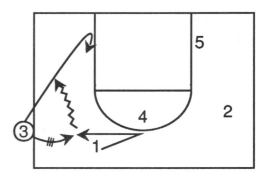

A

Player #3 passes to #1 and cuts to the block. Player #1 takes the ball on the dribble to the wing.

B

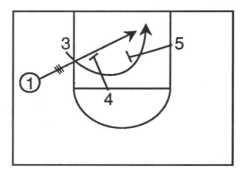

Player #4, positioned at the free throw line, screens down for #3. As #3 is curling, #5 steps up to screen #3's defender again for a potential lob pass.

C

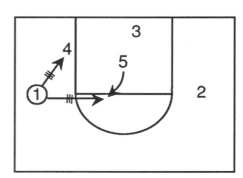

If any of the defenders help on #3, either #4 or #5 are open inside.

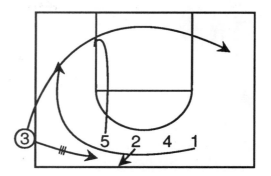

A

Player #1 curls around the stack to the ball-side wing, #5 drops to the block, #2 cuts hard to receive the inbound pass and #3 cuts underneath #5.

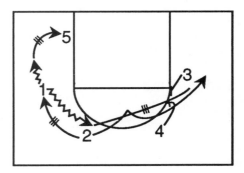

B

Player #2 passes to #1, who engages #5 in a two-player game. If that is cut off, #2 receives a double screen from #3 and #4 for the skip pass over the top from #1.

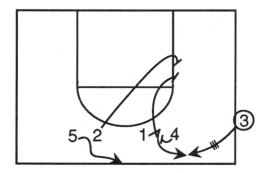

A

Player #4 turns and screens for #1, and #1 receives the inbound pass from #3. Players #2 and #4 slide down below the free throw line to set a double screen for #3. Player #5 is the safety in case #1 is not open to receive the inbound pass.

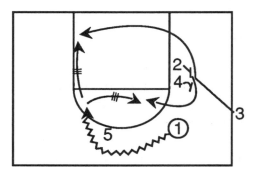

B

Player #1 takes the ball on the dribble off of the screen set by #5, and turns the corner to the basket if possible. Player #3 shuffle cuts through the lane looking for a pass off of the double screens set by #2 and #4. Player #5 turns and screens again for #1 after #3 has cut.

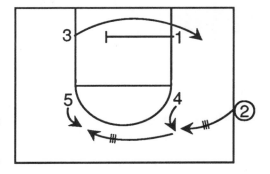

A

Player #2 inbounds to #4, while #1 screens for #3 in the low post. Player #4 reverses the ball to #5 on the perimeter.

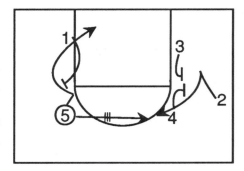

B

After #5 receives the pass, #3 and #4 turn to set a double screen for #2, who looks for a potential jump shot. After #5 passes to #2, #1 steps up the lane for a quick backscreen for #5, who shuffle cuts to the hoop.

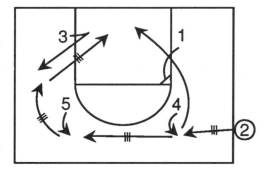

C

Option: The play is aligned the same as in Diagram A, exept #1 does not screen for #3. The ball is reversed to #4, then #5.

Player #5 passes to #3 as #1 sets a backscreen for #4, who cuts through the lane for a layup.

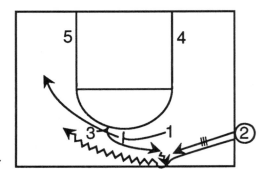

A

Player #1 screens away for #3. Player #2 inbounds to #3, then follows the pass and takes a handoff from #3. As #2 dribbles the ball toward the wing, #5 flashes above the free throw line for a feed from #2.

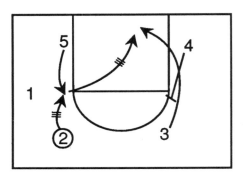

B

As #5 comes to receive the pass from #2, #4 comes out on the court to backscreen #3's defender for a layup.

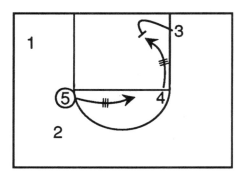

C

If #5 cannot feed #3 for the layup, a pass should be made to #4. Player #3 then reverse pivots and posts up as #4 takes the ball on the dribble to the wing looking to feed the post.

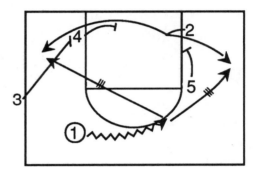

A

Player #4 screens down for #1, who receives the inbound pass.

B

After #1 receives the pass, #5 screens down on the weak side for #2 (who is the primary scorer in this play). As an option for #2, #4 steps into the middle of the lane and #3 comes to the baseline to set a staggered screen for #2 on the other side. Player #2 can go either way to receive the pass from #1 for the scoring opportunity.

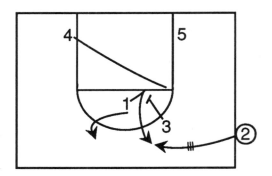

A

Player #3 screens down for #1, who pops out for the inbound pass. Player #3 then steps out on the perimeter opposite #1 and #4 flashes from the opposite block to the ball-side free throw line.

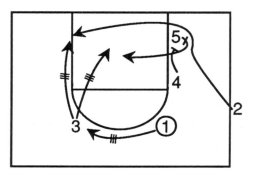

B

Player #1 reverses the ball to #3, while #2 receives a baseline screen from #5 at the block. Player #2 cuts across the lane looking for a layup. Player #4 then screens #5, who circles into the middle of the lane for a pass from #3.

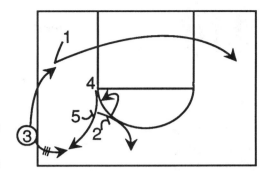

A

Players #2 and #5 screen for #4 so that #4 can receive the inbound pass. Player #1 cuts hard through the lane to the opposite wing. Player #5 steps out on the perimeter and #2 stays at the free throw line

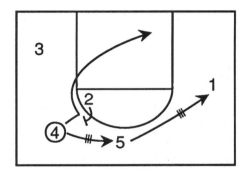

B

Player #4 reverses the ball to #5, who passes to #1. Player #2 steps out and screens for #4 as #3 steps to the wing.

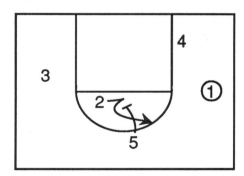

C

After #4 is screened by #2, #5 screens down for #2 for the jump shot. (This is a variation of pick-the-picker.)

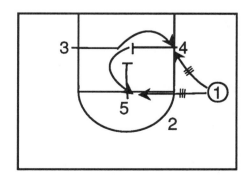

D

If neither of these options creates a scoring opportunity, #4 turns and screens for #3, who had tightened up to the lane, and #5 screens for #4 for a jump shot.

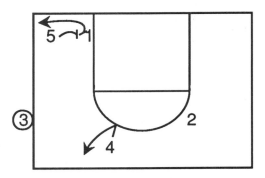

A

This is a good play to isolate a guard who has the ability to post up inside.

Player #5 screens in for #1. Player #4 cuts and then returns to become a safety out in front of the ball.

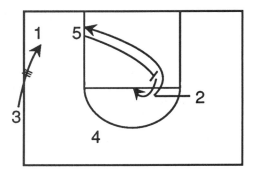

B

Player #3 inbounds to #1 as #5 continues diagonally up the lane to screen for #2, who cuts to the ball-side block for the post-up. Player #5 screens, then turns back to the ball for a potential shot at the free throw line.

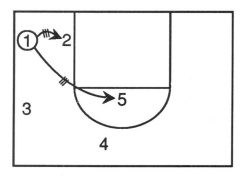

C

The options include the pass to #2 in the low post and the pass to #5 for a jump shot.

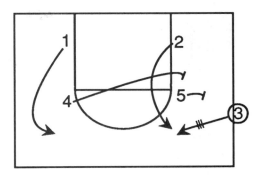

A

Player #2 cuts from the ball-side block to receive the inbound pass, while #4 cuts across the lane to set up a double screen with #5. Player #1 comes out to the opposite wing to empty out the weak side.

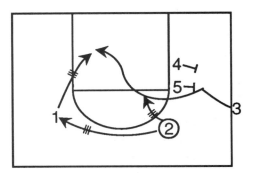

B

After #2 has received the pass from #3, the first look is to try to hit #3 on a cut over the double screen. If that is not open, #3 continues to the low post. If #2 passes to #1, #1 looks for #3 posting up inside.

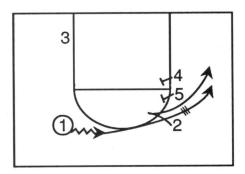

C

Option: After #2 passes to #1, #2 can flare to the weak side for a skip pass from #1 for a three-point shot.

D

Option: Player #4 steps to top of the key after the double screen while #5 drops to the block for a post up. Three players now are on the perimeter and two players are posting up inside. The offense can be initiated from here. Player #3 can pop out to the perimeter to clear out the defensive help as #5 posts alone in the lane area.

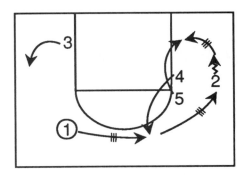

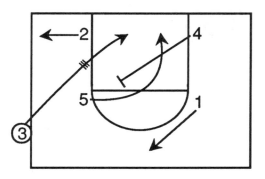

A

Player #3 slaps the ball and #2 cuts to the corner looking for a pass. Player #5 is just above the free throw line facing the ball, while #4 comes from the weakside block to back-screen #5's defender for a lob pass to the basket.

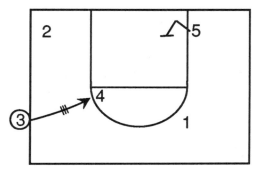

B

If #5 does not receive the lob pass, #4 can catch the inbound pass from #3 and then look to make a post feed to #5.

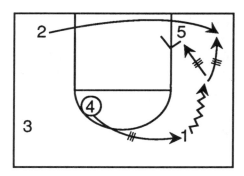

C

If #4 cannot pass the ball to #5, the pass is made to #1, who dribbles the ball to the wing. Player #5 posts up on the ball-side block. Player #2 runs along the baseline underneath #5 to the corner. Player #1 can pass the ball to either player.

123

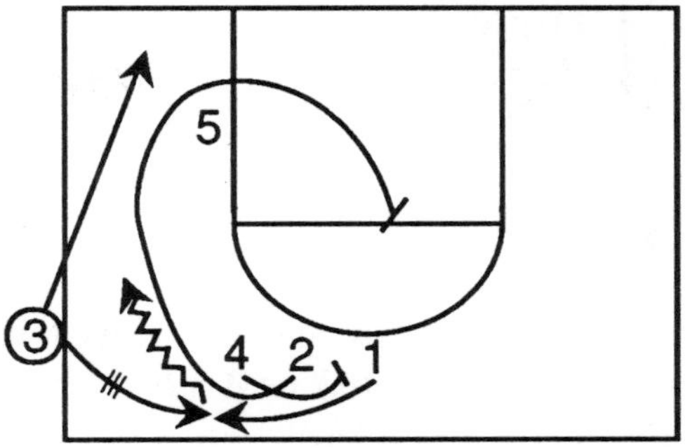

A

This play results in a lob pass out of a unique setup.

Players #4, #2 and #1 line up above the top of the key. Player #2 loops around #4 to begin the play. Player #4 then screens for #1, who receives the inbound pass. Player #1 dribbles the ball to the wing while #2 cuts underneath #5. Player #4 begins to circle around toward the lane.

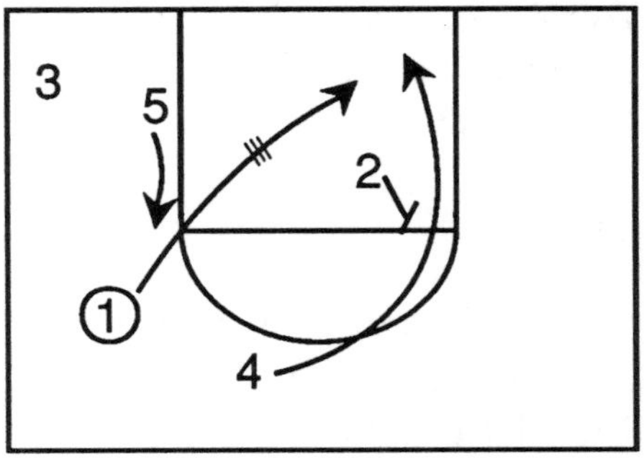

B

Player #2 backscreens for #4 for the lob pass from #1 as #5 slides up the lane to move the defender away from the action. Player #2 steps to the ball after screening in case the lob pass is not available.

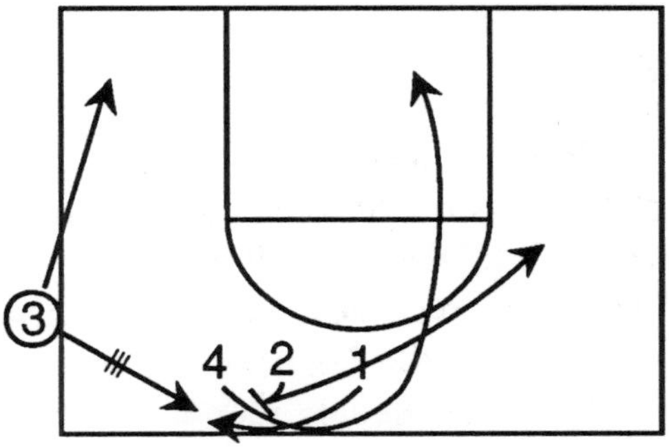

C

Option: Player #2 backscreens for #4. Player #1 receives the inbound pass, while #2 steps to the opposite wing to clear the defense.

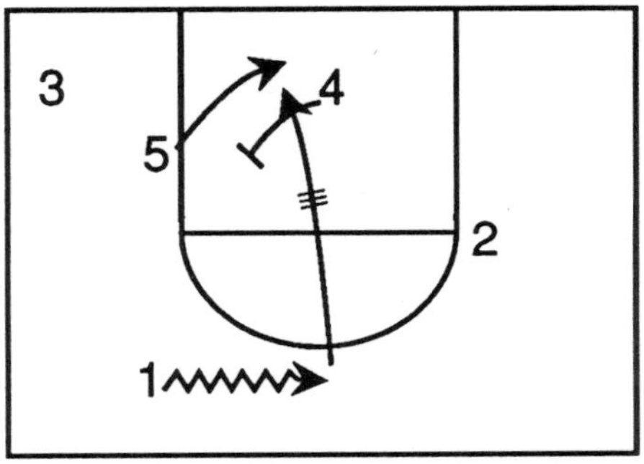

D

If #4 is not open for the lob from #1, #4 turns up the lane and screens for #5 for a second opportunity for a lob pass.

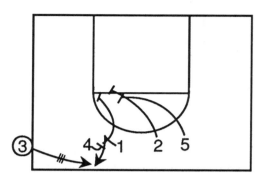

A

Player #4 screens for #1, who receives the inbound pass. Players #2, #4 and #5 all go to triple screen for #3.

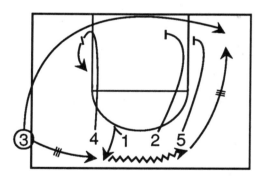

B

Player #3 takes the defender down and then curl cuts over the screens for a pass from #1 and looks for the shot.

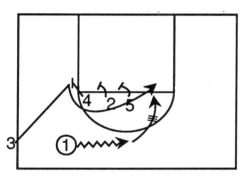

A

Player #1 cuts toward halfcourt and receives the inbound pass, then takes the ball on the dribble to the other wing. Players #2, #4 and #5 all go to the baseline to set staggered screens for #3, who runs the baseline for a return pass.

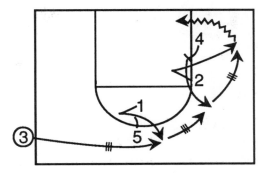

A

This is meant to be an isolation play for #2. It is a "quick hitter."

Player #5 screens for #1, who receives the inbound pass. At the same time, #4 steps up and backscreens for #2, who flares out to the wing. Player #4 then steps out to receive the pass from #1, and in turn passes to #2 for the clearout.

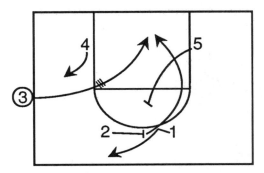

A

This is a quick lob pass intended to catch the defense off-guard.

Player #2 screens for #1, while #5 cuts from the opposite block to quickly screen for #2 for a potential lob pass to the basket. Player #4 steps toward the ball as a safety and to draw the defense away from the lane.

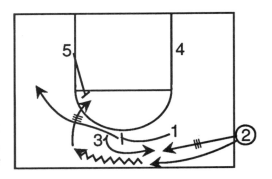

A

Player #1 screens for #3, and #2 inbounds to #3. Player #2 then follows the pass and takes a handoff from #3. As #2 dribbles the ball toward the wing, #5 flashes above the free throw line for a feed from #2.

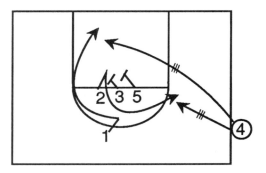

B

After #5 receives the pass, #4 comes out on the court to backscreen #3's defender for a layup.

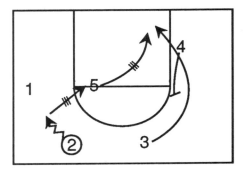

A

Players #2, #3 and #5 line up in a stack along the free throw line. Player #1 cuts hard to the basket for a possible lob. Players #3 and #5 pick for #2, who curls around them.

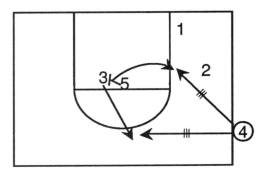

B

If #2 is not open for a short jumper, player #5 screens for #3, who pops to the top of the key. Player #5 then turns toward the ball for the pass. The inbounder can pass to either #3 or #5.

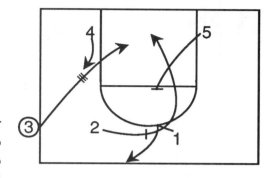

A

Player #2 screens for #1. Player #5 cuts from the opposite block to quickly screen for #2 for a lob pass to the basket. Player #4 steps toward the ball as a safety and to draw the defense away from the lane.

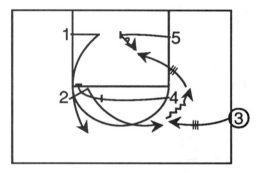

A

This play attempts to isolate the center in the low post.

Players #4 and #5 screen across the lane for #1 and #2. Player #3 inbounds the ball to #2. Player #1 sets up the defender as if preparing to cut across the lane, but instead cuts toward the top of the key and comes off of #4's screen. Player #2 brings the ball to #5's side for a two-player game.

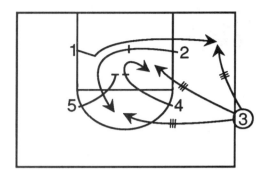

A

This is a standard and effective play to run if you have a guard who is a good shooter and the defense you are playing against does not like to switch.

Player #2 screens for #1 across the lane. Player #1 continues along the baseline. Players #4 and #5 both screen down to screen for #2, which is another variation of pick-the-picker.

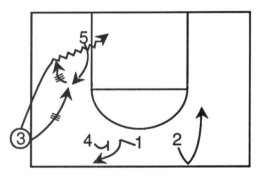

A

This is a very old play — and very effective!

Player #5 flashes hard to receive a pass from #3, then #3 follows the pass for a quick return pass from #5. Player #3 may be able to take the ball to the basket for a layup.

This play is most effective when the defense is in a tough denial mode and is caught overplaying. This play can be run anywhere along the sideline, but is most effective when run away from the basket toward the halfcourt line.

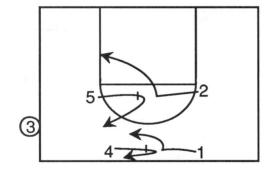

A

This is perhaps the safest alignment from which to inbound the ball anywhere along the sideline, and therefore can be effective while trying to protect a lead late in the game.

Both #1 and #2 read their defensive players as #4 and #5 set screens for them. The two guards set up the defense and rub their defenders off of the screens to find an open area. Players #4 and #5 also find open areas as they come back to the ball, leaving four potential receivers.

Get into the game!

Masters Press has a complete line of books on
basketball and other sports to help coaches
and participants alike "master their game."

All of our books are available at better bookstores
or by calling Masters Press at 1-800-722-2677, or
317-298-5706. Catalogs available upon request.

Our basketball books include the following:

Five-Star Basketball

Edited by Ed Schilling and Howard Garfinkel

Join the audience for some of the greatest lectures in the history of
the legendary Five-Star basketball camp. Superstar coaches such as
Bob Knight, Chuck Daly, Rick Pitino, George Raveling and Mike Fra-
tello, as well as former star players such as Clark Kellogg and Terry
Tyler, share insights and advice that not only will improve basketball
skills, but help anyone achieve his or her potential on and off the court.

$14.95 • paper • 224 pages • b/w photos

ISBN: 0-940279-58-4

Conditioning for Basketball

By Matt Brzycki and Shaun Brown

Shaun Brown, the strength coach at the University of Kentucky, and
Matt Brzycki, the strength coach at Princeton University, draw from
nearly 20 years of experience in strength training and conditioning in
this book on strength training principles, program design, general and
specific conditioning, conditioning drills, nutrition and flexibility. Includes a conditioning program for the entire year. Foreword by Kentucky basketball coach Rick Pitino.

$12.95 • paper • 160 pages • b/w photos

ISBN: 0-940279-56-8

Coaching Basketball: The Official Centennial Volume of the National Association of Basketball Coaches

Edited by Jerry Krause

The ultimate reference book for all basketball coaches, this is the compilation of more than 130 articles by the nation's leading coaches at the professional, college and high school levels. No coach who takes his or her job seriously should be without it!

Includes the following chapters:

★ The Birth of the Game (James Naismith)

★ Thoughts on Coaching (Al McGuire)

★ Daily Practice (John Wooden)

★ Organization of Practice and Season (Chuck Daly)

★ Timeouts and Substitutions (Dean Smith)

★ Tips on Scouting (Rick Majerus)

★ Anatomy of a Rebound (George Raveling)

★ Post Play (John Thompson)

★ Zone Attacks (Jud Heathcote)

★ Pressing Principles (Jerry Tarkanian)

★ Match-up Press Defense (Rick Pitino)

★ A Game Plan (Bob Knight)

$24.95 • cloth • 384 pages • diagrams throughout
ISBN: 0-940279-29-0

Five-Star Basketball Drills

Edited by Howard Garfinkel

Includes 131 of the best conditioning and skill drills from Five-Star, the nation's premier basketball camp. A star-studded galaxy of coaches, including Mike Krzyzewski, Rick Pitino and Bob Knight, share the activities that have proven successful year after year at Five-Star.

$12.95 • paper • 256 pages • fully illustrated
ISBN: 0-940279-22-3

MASTERS PRESS

DEAR VALUED CUSTOMER,

Masters Press is dedicated to bringing you timely and authoritative books for your personal and professional library. As a leading publisher of sports and fitness books, our goal is to provide you with easily accessible information on topics that interest you written by the most qualified authors. You can assist us in this endeavor by checking the box next to your particular areas of interest.

We appreciate your comments and will use the information to provide you with an expanded and more comprehensive selection of titles.

Thank you very much for taking the time to provide us with this helpful information.

Cordially,
Masters Press

Areas of interest in which you'd like to see Masters Press publish books:

☐ COACHING BOOKS
Which sports? What level of competition?

☐ INSTRUCTIONAL/DRILL BOOKS
Which sports? What level of competition?

☐ FITNESS/EXERCISE BOOKS
   ☐ Strength—Weight Training
   ☐ Body Building
   ☐ Other

☐ REFERENCE BOOKS
what kinds?

☐ BOOKS ON OTHER
Games, Hobbies
or Activities

Are you more likely to read a book or watch a video-tape to get the sports information you are looking for?

I'm interested in the following sports as a participant:

I'm interested in the following sports as an observer:

Please feel free to offer any comments or suggestions to help us shape our publishing plan for the future.

Name _____ Age _____

Address _____

City _____ State _____ Zip _____

Daytime phone number _____

BUSINESS REPLY MAIL

FIRST CLASS MAIL   PERMIT NO. 1317   INDIANAPOLIS IN

POSTAGE WILL BE PAID BY ADDRESSEE

MASTERS PRESS

2647 WATERFRONT PKY EAST DR

INDIANAPOLIS IN 46209-1418

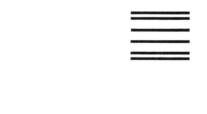